WORK IN

WORK IN WORSHIP

an anthology of material suitable for worship concerned with industry, commerce and all forms of work

compiled by

CAMERON BUTLAND

sponsored by

The Industrial Christian
Fellowship and the Oxford
Institute for Church and Society

HODDER AND STOUGHTON
LONDON SYDNEY AUCKLAND TORONTO

British Library Cataloguing in Publication Data

Work in worship: an anthology of material suitable
   for worship concerned with industry, commerce
   and all forms of work. – (Hodder Christian
   paperbacks)
   1. Prayer-books
   I. Butland, Cameron   II. Industrial Christian
   Fellowship   III. Oxford Institute for Church
   and Society
   242′.8   BV245

   ISBN 0-340-37402-0

COMMENDATION

by the Archbishop of Canterbury

Industry and commerce are today the scene of bitter division: between employer and employee, Union bureaucracy and rank and file, employed and unemployed. Crucial to these sharp divides is the gulf between the Church and the everyday world of work. Worship can be the focus for our private, Sunday lives only, depriving our workaday lives of their true godliness.

This excellent anthology is a timely attempt to bridge the gap between the worshipping Christian and the working Christian. Cameron Butland has carefully compiled and arranged a mass of material for use in public and private prayer which has work as its theme. I hope it will be widely used to help us to pray with our Lord: 'Thy kingdom come, thy will be done, on earth as it is in heaven.'

ROBERT CANTUAR

PREFACE

The anthology has been structured to serve two purposes. The first is to provide material for use by those who are compiling public acts of worship, the second for those who wish to have something on which to focus their own prayers in relation to their daily lives.

It is hoped that the structure of the anthology will make it easy for a selection of prayers, readings, hymns etc. to be used within existing forms of services to give an overall work-related theme to the service. It may be that just a particular prayer or hymn will be useful and the anthology is structured so as to make it simple to do this. However, the cross-reference for the anthology does provide a selection of service-plans which, together with the suggestions for 'using the experience of work', means that the anthology can provide the form as well as the content of a service. This flexibility should enable the anthology to contribute to the creation of public worship in many different ways without imposing its own style upon the service.

The division may seem at first glance less well-suited to the second of the anthology's functions. Indeed it may be that one or more of the sections, such as 'Hymns and songs', may prove to be of little use to the Christian in private devotion. However, the anthology does contain much which could be of value to supplement the existing routine of prayer of a Christian. For those who wish to use the anthology regularly the 'Cross-reference' section does contain a plan to provide a daily manual of prayer and meditation. This may also provide a useful basis for a short time of prayer for small groups of Christians who meet together at work or for groups in a parish who meet after work.

The anthology is largely self-explanatory. However, the

'Unemployment' section needs some explanation. Why separate this material from the rest of the anthology? The reason is twofold. Firstly, it is to avoid any confusion within the other sections and secondly it is to draw attention to this material. It would be easy to include the material within the other sections and so in some sense hide it away. However, the gap between the Christian unemployed and the Christian at worship is but another dimension of the gap between the Christian at work and the Christian at worship. The material is thus aimed to be used by not only those who are unemployed but also by those who work.

Finally, it is important, I believe, to point to the inadequacies of this anthology. Its greatest strength and its most severe weakness is that it is breaking new ground. It is, as far as I know, the first of its kind, but it is my hope that it will not be the last. This is not to undervalue the content of the anthology – much of it is excellent – and yet I do not believe that it is the finest that can be produced. Rather I hope that the anthology will provide a useful resource for the immediate future but that it will at the same time challenge many to produce better prayers and better forms of worship to serve more fully the needs of Christian people.

*   *   *

I am greatly indebted to many people in putting together this anthology. Indeed I can claim no credit for the original idea of it, which came from the ICF (the Industrial Christian Fellowship). My involvement in the project was made possible only by Alastair Redfern and the Oxford Institute for Church and Society, who approached me to compile the anthology. Both John Davis of ICF and Alastair Redfern have been a constant encouragement to me and I gratefully acknowledge the part they have played in making this anthology possible.

It would be wrong not to acknowledge also the help given to me by Paul Brett, of the Church of England's General Synod Board for Social Responsibility, who put me in touch with many people, and by Miss Owen, the Librarian of Sion College, who kindly let me use the archives of the ICF.

Lastly, I must thank all those who took the time and trouble to reply to my many letters, who sent me material, and all who have allowed me to use their work. I sincerely thank all who have helped me in any way.

CONTENTS

12

INTRODUCTION

THE NEED FOR AN
ANTHOLOGY – BRIDGING THE GAP

'We know, when we stop to think, that we are dependent upon industry, and yet we are unable to affirm industrial life as being of real worth. This is a basic sickness at the heart of our society, a failure in our fundamental attitudes.'

'Having spent ten years in industrial chaplaincy I am acutely aware of the very large gap which seems to divide people's Church-based Christianity from almost everything else they are involved in. The result is the loss of effective Christian influence in large areas of human activity. Even when we bring worship and work together it is in "church" and many people will have to do a spiritual and mental somersault before they see the need to apply Christian truth to their own areas of understanding.'

The first extract is from an address by the Bishop of Ripon to his diocesan synod and the second is part of a letter written to the compiler of this book by an industrial chaplain. Both reflect the lack of any anthology of material for worship that might help to bridge the gap between the Church and the everyday world of work. This anthology is, as far as I know, the first to be devoted solely to the needs and interests of those who work in industry and commerce, and as such it is long overdue.

The churches have made considerable efforts over the last thirty-five years to stress the Christian's proper role in work. The growth and development of industrial mission teams has done much to re-root the Christian voice in the everyday lives of working men and women. Much valuable work is done by them and there is much to be grateful for in their work. There has been some growth in the numbers of special services designed for those who work. These are all encouraging signs that the Church is taking seriously the challenge of worshipping in the world.

And yet, much still needs to be done. For there is still a large gap. I do not mean the gap between the Christian and non-Christian at work, but rather the gap between the Christian at work and the Christian at worship. If the worship of the Church ignores the everyday lives of the congregations it is denying their part in the creative work of God, it denies that God is active outside the walls of his Church, it denies that the Christian has anything distinctive to say about the proper ordering of working relationships, and most of all, it denies everything in life which is not church-based. Small wonder that in some places the number of church attendances continues to decline if worship is focused only on the interests of the Church and not on the needs of those who come to worship.

To many this analysis of the Church's worship must read like an attack on the traditional forms of service, a desire for change at all costs, pointing merely to the drab everyday world whilst ignoring the proper celebration of the worship of God. Nothing could be further from the truth. This anthology, whilst recognising the gap that exists between the Christian at work and the Christian at worship, seeks only to encourage worship to be a true offering of 'worth' to God. As Christians, we should not be conformed to the world but should work with God to transform it and become like God's Kingdom on earth. We already say this week by week in the Lord's Prayer and yet there is a place for this link to be made more overtly in the prayers, readings, hymns and, indeed, in the way in which we worship.

What is the basis for this affirmation of the everyday world of work? The basis is to be found in the life, death and resurrection of Jesus. It is to be found in the writings and sermons of many leading Christians, past and present. Most importantly, it is to be found in the everyday lives of Christian people.

We believe as Christians that God was uniquely present amongst his creation in the life of Jesus as the Word made flesh. So anyone who looks upon Jesus can recognise God and his activity in the world. Jesus's mission was to bring in God's Kingdom on earth by reconciling man to God. So his ministry was characterised by a concern for all people, especially those who were denied any place in society by the Jewish law. In this, then, God was active in caring for the needs of all people, and it is on the cross, where we believe God himself suffered, experiencing the total humiliation and pain of humanity. Thereby the resurrection redeemed all this creation in its suffering, which had separated it from him. This redemption and the giving of the Holy Spirit marked the beginning of God's Kingdom, and proclaimed that God was active for all time within his whole Creation.

Thus for Christians their everyday lives, leisure and work are not something separate from their faith. This is a central truth of the Gospel and one which has been constantly repeated by Christian writers.

'God has to be discovered in the situation,' wrote Margaret Kane in her book, *Theology in an Industrial Society*. 'It is in and through the people we meet, the day-to-day happenings of life . . . that God comes to us.' Writing this in the mid-1970s, Kane was echoing the words of the Anglican theologian, F. D. Maurice, from over a century earlier. For Maurice thought of the Kingdom of Heaven as 'the great existing reality' and that God's Kingdom was not limited to the Church but that it embraced the whole of creation. The consequence of Maurice's theology therefore was to see all work as made holy through God's presence, in the ministry of Jesus and through the work of the Holy Spirit. Thus creation and redemption for him already existed within the affairs of the world.

William Temple, influenced by the writing of Maurice, saw the need to bridge the gap between the Christian at work and the Christian at worship, quite unlike any Archbishop of Canterbury before him. In his book, *Christianity and Social Order*, published in 1942, Temple argued that the Church, and Christians, not only had a right to involvement in the affairs of the workplace but also had a duty to become involved. He said that all thinking must begin with God, for 'man is created for fellowship in the family of God, fellowship first with God, and through that with all other God's children.' As children of God therefore all have a social responsibility and a duty to question the world, in order to see if it matches this fellowship with God.

The lives of Christians are therefore inevitably bound up with the society in which they live and work. For worship to ignore this is to create a divide and to produce an inner conflict within each Christian. Worship should rather be a true offering of the whole person, of his or her life and work, to God – a true celebration of what God has done and is doing, and a true reflection upon the Christian's distinctive role within society.

The various sections of the anthology provide some of the tools for the vocalisation of this proper worship, and yet as they remain on the pages of this book they are worthless. It is only when they become the means by which Christians can make the link between their work and their faith that they become of true worth, become true worship.

USING THE EXPERIENCE OF WORK – THE GAP BRIDGED

The gap between the Christian at work and the Christian at worship can be bridged in many ways, but the one vital link is the Christian. For the Christian in worship brings all the experience of work to offer to God as part of the whole person. The starting point for worship is thus not in clever prayers woven into a unified structure but rather the experience of the Christian at work which is able to relate to the whole service or just to some part of it.

Services with a 'work' theme

This is the easiest and most obvious way to relate worship to daily work without disrupting the usual pattern of worship. The inclusion of prayers, readings and hymns, together with a related sermon, does provide an effective focus for the worship, and yet there is more that can be done. There is a danger in a very word-orientated service, on the theme of work, of missing the point – for work is experienced, it is part of everyday life and so for most people it is rarely put into words. There is also the danger that the only experience to be contributed in this type of service is that of the leader and so the experience of Christians in the congregation may not be adequately drawn out.

The most successful way, I believe, to overcome this situation is to involve the members of the Church in creating the worship not only in the prayers but also in other parts of the service. In a leaflet produced by the Church of Scotland Home Board, *A Festival of Daily Work*, there are suggestions as to how this may be achieved. For example, instead of a sermon two or three members of the congregation could contribute short addresses attempting to say how the Christian faith supports, guides and challenges them within the sphere of their employment; what Christian insights are helpful in their daily work; how they may see their Christian responsibilities as shop stewards or supervisors, managers, sales representatives, tradesmen or training officers; what the difficult areas are for Christians in their places of work, and where especially we are to seek God's help and guidance. Or, to move away from purely words, several people could bring items from their work and present them as part of the offertory at the Communion Service. There are also many excellent posters, some of which could be used to focus the service on different aspects of work.

These are a few suggestions but it is true to say that anything that can involve members of the congregation expressing in some way their own experience of work is likely to broaden the worship and help to bridge the gap.

Festivals of daily work

An industrial festival is a more ambitious approach to bridging the gap and yet it is potentially more successful. A weekend or, more practically, a day's festival culminating in an act of worship can help to explore the experience of work for the Christian more fully than a dozen special services. The Home Board of the Methodist Church has produced an excellent leaflet, *Industrial Festivals! ... What! At my church?*, which provides much practical advice as to how to arrange such a festival.

What are the benefits of such festivals? First, it can provide a context in which Christians are encouraged to explore their own experience. This may be done through photographic displays, displays of the products of local firms, film strips and talks. The very act of putting together such a festival will necessarily involve the members of the church in pooling their experience. Second, it is a chance to draw in industrial chaplains and leading Christian figures from industry and commerce to explore various themes – personal witness at work, ethical behaviour in business, the responsibilities of the Christian worker, God's activity in the world, proper working relationships – these are but a few possibilities. Third, such festivals can draw in those who are not committed to any church and so show to many that Christians are concerned about the problems of everyday living. Fourthly, a festival can provide the setting for worship, which is the climax of all the talks and exhibitions. The Christian having already spent some time considering how faith is related to daily work is then, hopefully, in a better position to offer that part of life as true 'worth' to God.

A festival may seem a daunting task and yet there are many willing to help – industrial chaplains, local boards for social responsibility and for home mission, together with the resources which already exist in the congregations worshipping Sunday by Sunday in the churches. Towards the end of this book there is a section entitled 'Further Resources' (pages 185–194) which would be helpful in arranging such a festival.

Informal acts of worship

Because of its very nature it is, of course, difficult to provide more than the broadest outlines and suggestions for the conduct of informal acts of worship. However, in the right setting, the informal does have advantages over the formal in expressing for particular groups of people at particular times their own part in God's creation. This is nearly always only possible in small groups, for with large numbers there needs to be some more formal approach, and so, in terms of structure, this type may not be suitable for a main church service.

One industrial mission team wrote to me offering several outlines of informal worship. The following is an example: 'The leader played the headlines from the BBC News, taped only minutes before, as an introduction. They reflected where God's world was today and helped us make the link into the world at the outset of our worship.' This was followed by a 'shortened and informalised form of the Eucharist' which included 'a reading related to God's continuing love for the world. In place of a sermon, each person was asked to share something he/she was celebrating in life, work or leisure, something of joy, thanksgiving or hope.' The service ended when they 'broke bread/took wine in a circle', and finished by singing an appropriate hymn.

The use of a tape recording is but one way of focusing attention on God's activity in the world – newspapers, photographs, contemporary songs, items from various jobs can all be used to provoke discussion and guide meditation. Similarly, the leader could use a few sentences from the Bible, extracts from the life of a particular Christian, list local institutions and firms – anything which serves to reinforce the subject of the worship. It seems important though that this type of service should allow Christians not only to reflect on what has been said and seen, but also to make the link with their own experience.

Further suggestions for this type of worship may be found in the 'Cross-Reference' section of this book (see under 'Service Plans' ix and x, on pages 173–174).

The gap bridged

These suggestions provide but the barest guidelines as to how this might be achieved. The key is the Christian, and so the object is to construct a service which can enable the Christian to make the link between faith and everyday life.

CAMERON BUTLAND

ANTHOLOGY

PRAYERS

(a) General
(b) Confession
(c) Commitment
(d) Thanksgiving

PRAYERS

(a) General

1. Lord Jesus Christ alive and at large in your world, help us to follow and find you there today in the places where we meet people, spend money and make plans. Take us as disciples of your Kingdom, to see through your eyes, to hear the questions you are asking, to welcome all men with your trust and truth, and to change the things that contradict God's love, by the power of the cross, and by the freedom of your spirit. Amen.

2. Almighty God, sustainer of daily life and work, and provider of all our needs. Open our hearts to your creative power so that we might know your will, praise your name, and share your vision for the creation of your Kingdom. In the name of your Son, Jesus Christ our Lord. Amen.

3. O God, the Father of all mankind, we beseech you to inspire us with such love, truth and equity that, in all our dealings one with another, we may show forth our brotherhood in you; for the sake of Jesus Christ our Lord. Amen.

4. O Lord, renew us and draw us up to yourself, that our work may not be unto us a burden but a delight: and give us such a mighty love for you, who did yourself work as a craftsman in wood. O let us not serve you in our daily work in a spirit of resentment but with cheerfulness and willingness, co-operating with you in your work of creation. And this we ask in your name. Amen.

5. Lord of all things in heaven and earth, the land and the sea and all that therein is, take from us, we humbly

beseech you, the spirit of gain and covetousness and give us the spirit of service, so that none may want, but each according to his need may share in your bountiful liberality; for the love of your only Son, Jesus Christ our Lord. Amen.

6. O God, whose glory the heavens declare and whose handiwork the firmament showeth, deliver us, we beseech you, from the dominion of mammon, and grant that all labour and handicraft may be established in justice and become a work of ministry in your kingdom of grace; through Jesus Christ our Lord. Amen.

7. God our Father,
open our mind to see ourselves as you see us,
or at least to see ourselves as others see us.
Save us from want of purpose;
from lack of concern for others;
from self interest and seeking for status.
Give us generous hearts and the will to support those
    around us.

Lord Jesus of Nazareth
Support us in our work.
Save us from complacency;
from lack of conscience and loss of integrity.
Give us such understanding
that we recognise the truth in other people.
Give us power to overcome all that is unacceptable to
    you.

Holy Spirit, power of Creation.
Enliven our work and our leisure.
Restore the confidence of those who have no work.
Inspire our efforts to relieve unemployment.
Save us from envy and malice,
From selfishness, dissension and strife.
Remove prejudice and ignorance

And encourage us to support each other, at work and
at home. Amen.

8. O God our Father, who hast raised up for us many
benefactors, known and unknown, remembered and
forgotten, whose harvest we today are reaping: Make us
also faithful in this our day, that we may sow a generous
harvest, which others shall reap hereafter; through
Jesus Christ our Lord. Amen.

9. Give us, O Lord, a steadfast heart,
which no unworthy thought can drag downwards;
an unconquered heart, which no tribulation can wear
out;
an upright heart, which no unworthy purpose may
tempt aside;
Give us understanding to know thee,
diligence to seek thee,
wisdom to find thee,
and a faithfulness that may finally embrace thee;
through Jesus Christ our Lord. Amen.

10. O Lord our God, who has called us to serve you in the
midst of the world's affairs
when we stumble, hold us;
when we fall, lift us up;
when we are hard pressed by evil, deliver us;
when we turn from what is good, turn us back;
and bring us at last to your glory.

O Lord, support us all the day long of this troublous life,
until the shadows lengthen, and the evening comes, and
the busy world is hushed, the fever of life is over, and
our work done. Then, Lord, in your mercy, grant us safe
lodging, a holy rest and peace at the last; through Jesus
Christ our Lord. Amen.

11. Help me Lord to see myself as dependent upon others.
What does it matter where I work, what my job is?

You spoke of yourself as the cornerstone of the
 building.
I desire just to be part of that building, unseen and
 unknown but playing my part with everyone else.

Teach me the value of work done in the service of
 others;
Teach me the value of work done in humility;
Teach me the value of work done in self-giving love;
That all I do may be done to your glory. Amen.

12. We acknowledge the personal significance we find in our
own work;
 the contribution we make in our work to the pattern
 of community life;
 our opportunities through voluntary groups to extend
 this into our spare time;

We offer this day's work, what we will do with others
 either in harmony or under tension, and what we will
 do alone,
 both what will be recognised, and what will be done
 secretly,
to be a sacrifice of thanksgiving for this day.

13. Teach me Lord, to let others help me.
Teach me to delegate, to trust.
That which I do, let's face it, is not so important.
Doing it alone makes me FEEL important . . .

Teach me, Lord, to stop, and look, and listen,
 To be still in the mind when I stop.
 To see beauty when I look.
 To hear more when I listen.

14. Lord, the world in which I live is so busy,
 There is so much to do.
 All my effort and attention is demanded.

I am pushed and pulled,
Travelling to and fro,
Cramming too much into too little time.
The minutes, the hours and the days are just too full,
   too busy.
Bring me your peace.
Bring me your quiet.
Bring me your love.

Lord, take away my tensions, fears and greed,
Stop me wanting more and more.
Let me take time to look beyond myself,
Let me look round and notice others,
That I might see them in their need.
Give me a heart to care and love,
That in others I might find your peace,
That there I might find your quiet,
And that I might show your love. Amen.

15. Suffer me never to think that I have knowledge enough
   to need no teaching,
wisdom enough to need no correction,
talents enough to need no grace,
goodness enough to need no progress,
humility enough to need no repentance,
devotion enough to need no quickening,
strength sufficient without thy Spirit;
lest, standing still, I fall back for evermore.

16. O Lord, remember not only the men and women of
goodwill, but also those of ill will. But do not remember
all the suffering they have inflicted on us; remember the
fruits we have bought, thanks to this suffering – our
comradeship, our loyalty, our humility, our courage,
our generosity, the greatness of heart which has grown
out of all this, and when they come to judgment, let all
the fruits which we have borne be their forgiveness.
Amen.

17. O Lord, help us in our work that we may show your love and care to our fellow-workers. Teach us the lesson that we are no more important than those who are at the bottom of the heap. Teach us to value the work of the cleaner, the floor sweeper, the security guard and night watchman. Let us never be so consumed with ambition that we use people for our own ends, but let us always be guided by your words, 'do unto others, as you would like them to do to you.' To the Father who creates and the Spirit who enlivens. Amen.

18. Lord, we pray for our fellow-workers, that there may be fair dealing between everybody, that our work may be good and that we may be proud of it. Make us patient with those people who make our job difficult because of temper, mistakes, awkwardness or selfishness. Teach us also that we can make others work harder through our own thoughtlessness. So help us to see what we can put right, to speak where we can sympathise, to feel for other people in their troubles, that we may remain close to you in other men's needs. Through Jesus Christ and the Holy Spirit, fellow workers in your creation. Amen.

19. Lord God Almighty, your Son Jesus Christ worked amongst men as a carpenter and went out with the fishermen. You know what it is to be worried and concerned to get the job done in time. You know what it feels like to be cold and wet, waiting with nothing to do. Keep us mindful always of your love and strength through the power of your Holy Spirit, and so teach us to give sympathy and help towards our fellow workers at all times and especially during the bad times. Amen.

20. Almighty Father, who by your Son, Jesus Christ, has sanctified labour to the welfare of mankind: Prosper, we pray, the industries of this land and all those who are engaged therein; that, shielded in all their temptations and dangers, and receiving a due reward of their

labours, they may praise you by living according to your
will; through Jesus Christ our Lord. Amen.

21. God, who created man in your image to be a maker and
craftsman, and in the joy of creation to be a mirror of
triune majesty:
Endow us with a passion to serve the science and art of
architecture with a perfect integrity; and grant that none
of those whose truth is in their craft may miss the true
knowledge of you, whose truth is in your Son, Jesus
Christ our Lord. Amen.

22. O God, who hast bound us together in this bundle of
life, give us grace to understand how our lives depend
upon the courage, the industry, the honesty and the
integrity of our fellow-men; that we may be mindful of
their needs, grateful for their faithfulness, and faithful in
our responsibilities to them, through Jesus Christ our
Lord. Amen.

23. Almighty God, who ordained that your Son, Jesus
Christ, should labour with his hands to supply his own
needs and the needs of others. Teach us that no labour is
without worth and all labour to which you call us is
divine, to the glory of your Holy Name. Amen.

24. A prayer for others:
    for those whose work is monotonous, dangerous,
        unpopular or done under urgent pressure;
    for those who want to work, but can find none;
    for those whose work is difficult to reconcile with
        their sense of human dignity;
    and for all on whose work we depend.

Stir up, O God, our wills and kindle our understanding;
that we may discern the way to a just society, where all
may work and all may find a fair reward, serving you
and one another in peace and goodwill, in the spirit of
Jesus Christ our Lord. Amen.

25. Lord, we pray for all those whose work is dangerous or unpleasant, giving thanks for their dedication and skill in working. Help us to be ever mindful of the difficulties of their work and never to denigrate what they do or to think that we are better than them. We pray this through your Son, Jesus Christ empowered by the Holy Spirit. Amen.

26. Lord, we pray for all assembled here, that wherever they work, in the home, in schools, in offices or factories they may be empowered by your Holy Spirit. May they work with integrity, seeking right relationships and an understanding of one another's problems. We ask this through your Son, Jesus Christ. Amen.

27. O Lord, we pray for all those working in all forms of commerce. May they seek by your help to serve others honestly with wisdom and judgment for the good of the community and nation. Help them to work together in unity and comradeship, being diligent in all their business that their work day by day may be offered to you as a prayer of their minds and hands. We ask this for the sake of Jesus Christ in whose name we sum up all our wants and needs. Amen.

28. O Almighty God, enlighten all merchants and tradesmen with the gift of your Holy Spirit, that they may consider, not what the world would sanction, but what your law commands. Prosper with your blessing all who are thus striving to regulate their dealings by the rule of truth and love: and if difficulty compass them in the world, quicken within them such a desire of laying up treasure in heaven as may cause them to accept your perfect will, teaching them so to use earthly things that they may become partakers of the true riches which cannot fail; through Jesus Christ our Lord. Amen.

29. Father, we pray for those who have the heavy burden of management. Help them always to be honest and fair in all dealings with those under them and with those who negotiate on their behalf. Help them to value their workforce as people with their own special gifts and never to be tempted to hold all power to themselves. Strengthen them to carry this burden. We ask this through your Son who has carried the burden for all mankind and through the Spirit who guides all in your ways. Amen.

30. O Almighty God, we acknowledge you to be the Creator of the Universe. We admit our total dependence upon your sustaining powers. We are grateful that man has been made in your image and thereby exercises creative skills and imagination. We appreciate that, by your grace, he has the ability to turn raw material into objects of value and beauty. May we, Lord, not forget our indebtedness to you, nor that all our creative efforts are performed to your honour and glory, now and for evermore. Amen.

31. O Lord God, your Creation holds within itself such promise for all your people. You have entrusted us with the stewardship of the earth and opened up before us a vision of what can be achieved. You have granted us a capacity to meet the needs of the deprived, to reach a measure of fulfilment through daily work and to use your resources responsibly. We pray that you may enable us to realise these hopes, so that, at the end, your Rule may indeed triumph for ever and ever. Amen.

32. We give thanks, O Lord, as stewards of your resources, for all our work. We give thanks for being able to work, for having work to do, for the blessings received and for the joy of fulfilling your creation. We pray that we may fulfil the trust you have granted us and that you may accept our work, our thanks and our love, now and evermore. Amen.

33. O Almighty God, who has entrusted this earth unto the children of men, and through your Son Jesus Christ has called us unto a heavenly citizenship; grant us, we humbly beseech you, such shame and repentance for the injustice that is in our midst, that fleeing unto you for pardon and for grace we may henceforth set ourselves to establish that city which has justice for its foundation and love for its law, whereof you are the Architect and Maker, through Jesus Christ, your Son, our Saviour. Amen.

34. O Blessed Jesus, who did teach us that the seed of your Kingdom is the Word of God, we beseech you to sow the seed of your own Life in our hearts, that by fellowship with you and with those with whom we labour, we may seek the coming of your Kingdom upon earth. Drive from our souls envy, jealousy and strife, that the earthly bread which we, under Divine Providence, do provide for your children, may be an offering acceptable to you. Grant that no evil will of men may prevent the just distribution of your gifts, but in equity and brotherhood your Will may be done for your Glory and the well-being of all your children, through the same Jesus Christ our Lord. Amen.

35. O Holy Wisdom of God, enlighten all men of science who search out the secrets of your creation, that their humility before nature may be matched by reverence towards you. Save us from misusing their labours that the forces they release may enrich the lives of all your children and that your Name may be hallowed both in the search for truth and in the use of power. Through Jesus Christ, our Lord. Amen.

36. O Lord Jesus Christ, who looked with compassion upon the multitude, awaken us to the shame of hunger, wretchedness and squalor that we may not rest until the world reflects your Glory and is filled with your Joy. Look mercifully on all who dwell in exile from beauty,

whose work is unrewarding and those who have no work; grant us so to use the gifts of science and of art that where men dwell there may be loveliness and where men work your Kingdom may be served. To the Father who creates and the Spirit who enlivens. Amen.

37. We thank God for the splendour of his creation and for the responsibility that he has given us in his world, and pray for our work in industry and commerce that he may guide us in the right use of all that is entrusted to us; and because the Church recognises its responsibility to minister in the world of work, we pray for all those commissioned by the Church to serve those who work in offices and factories throughout the land. Let us therefore have in mind the presence of God and pray that this service may be to his Glory. Through Jesus Christ our Lord. Amen.

38. Let us pray for the work of the Church's mission within technology, industry and commerce that within these spheres of man's activities, there shall be a full acknowledgment of Christ and his Kingdom. Amen.

39. Almighty and all-seeing God, we humbly beseech you to grant that, in whatsoever place we build, we may design with wisdom, strength and beauty, and that, out of a knowledge of the past, we may fulfil our obligations to the future: moreover, so strengthen us with your grace that, in all our projects, we may ever perceive and follow the more excellent way so that our works may find truth and righteousness in your sight and be of service to your people, even unto the end of the world, for Jesus's sake. Amen.

40. Our Father, in these hours of daylight we remember those who must awake that we may sleep: bless those who in the night watch over our lives and our homes, and guard all who carry on through the hours of darkness the restless commerce of man on land and sea. We

thank you for their faithfulness and sense of duty, we pray you to save us from any selfishness or luxury that may add to their nightly toil. Help us to understand how much we depend upon them for the safety of our loved ones and the comforts of life, that so we may think of them with love and gratitude, and help to make their burden lighter, for the sake of Jesus Christ our Lord. Amen.

41. Bless, O God, all who are engaged in industry and commerce; and, as your Son Jesus Christ plied tool and trade at Nazareth, so grant to all workers pride in their work, and a just reward, and the joy of serving you in serving their fellow men; through the same Jesus Christ our Lord. Amen.

42. Behold O Lord our striving after a truer and more abiding order. Grant us visions that bring back a lost glory to the earth and dreams that foreshadow the better order that you have prepared for us. Scatter every excuse of frailty and unworthiness; consecrate us all with a heavenly mission; open to us a clearer prospect of our work. Give us strength according to our daily need, through Jesus Christ our Lord. Amen.

43. Holy Spirit of fellowship and wisdom, make us to be comrades in deed as in name. Keep before our eyes the heavenly vision of your world as it might be. Put far from us the smallness of personal ambition, the pettiness of envy and the certainty that our way is always the best. Grant that others through our thinking and acting may find new freedom, new hope, new delight in living, new power in fulfilment in their work. And this we ask for the sake of Jesus Christ our Lord. Amen.

44. Hasten, O Lord, the day when men shall toil, not alone for their own gain, but for the common good; when all commerce shall be pure, all labour prayer, all work worship and when men shall rejoice in everything their hands have made and find increase of wealth in mutual service. Amen.

45. O God, grant us a vision of all places of work in our country, of offices and industries as places of righteousness, where none shall wrong his or her neighbour, where honour shall be given to everyone, and success be measured by service. May they be places of peace, where order rests not on force, but on the common consent of all those involved. Bless and guide all members of management and of the trade unions and all others who lead our industrial life, so that justice and compassion and your truth may inform all that they do for others. Through Jesus Christ, our Lord. Amen.

46. Grant us, O God,
   a vision of our world, fair as it might be;
   a world of justice where none prey on others;
   a world of plenty, where vice and poverty shall cease
      to fester;
   a world of brotherhood, where success shall be
      founded on service, and honour given to worth
      alone;
   a world of peace, where order shall not rest on force,
      but on the love of all for God and for each other.
      Amen.

47. O God our heavenly Father, we beseech you to hear us on behalf of all those who live by strength of arm or skill of hand. For men who face peril. For women who suffer pain. For those who till the earth, for those who tend machinery. For those whose business is in the deep waters, for sailors and seafarers. For those who work in offices and warehouses, for those who buy and sell. For those who labour at furnaces and in factories. For those who toil in mines. For those who keep house, for those who train children. For all who control, rule or employ. For all who are poor, and broken and oppressed. For all whose labour is without hope; for all whose labour is without honour. For all whose labour is without interest. For those who have too little leisure. For those who are underpaid. We pray for all women workers. We pray for all those who work in dangerous trades. For those who cannot find work, for those who have no home. For all prisoners and outcasts. For all who are sick, hungry or destitute. We pray, O Father, for all men everywhere, that it may please you to comfort, sustain, protect and support these and all others for whom we desire to pray, through Jesus Christ our Lord. Amen.

48. Eternal God, you created the world full of potential. We thank you that, in making us in your image, you made us capable of realising some of this potential by our work. Despite what we often say, we are glad there is work for us to do. So we cannot help praying for those without work; for the ill and the permanently injured; for those who leave school with no job to go to; for those who by their own or society's fault have become unemployable; those who find their skills no longer needed; for those who fear change; for those who face long-term unemployment.

We pray too, therefore, for those who bear the responsibility for choosing and directing the changes in our working lives: those in government, in management and in the trade unions; those engaged in training and the deployment of others; those involved in the reform of bargaining procedures. Save them equally from the idealism that ignores our competitiveness, and from the cynicism which assumes we shall never be generous. May their aim be not only to make us efficient, but, however impersonal a man's work may be, to make the place where he works a more personal place.

We pray for ourselves as Christians, that what we believe may find expression in our working day; that we may be good workers, and dependable in small things as well as large. If we have power, may we be straightforward in our use of it; if we are married, may we be fair to both our work and our home; when we have to com-

promise may it be in the general interest and not just our
own; and in all we do may we remember that we too
have a master in heaven. Amen.

49.   We give thanks to you, Almighty God, the Creator and
Sustainer of daily life, and Provider of materials for
man's use. Mindful that we are but stewards of your
creation, we pray that we may use your resources wisely
and for the good of all.
We give thanks to you, Jesus Christ, redeemer of all
man's activities, and the founder of a new creation on
earth. We pray that your presence with us in the Bread
and Wine may aid us to pursue our work in your strength
and according to your example.
We give thanks to you, Holy Spirit, provider of man's
various gifts.
We recognise that we need your inspiration and we ask
that you may lead us into the paths of truth and justice,
united in purpose and action.
We ask this through the one, holy and undivided Trinity. Amen.

50.   Lord, we believe this is your world but too often we
    lock ourselves away in churches,
We have prayed 'thy will be done' but in public life we
    have obeyed the world,
We have seen you challenged in the public life, but
    would not stand up and be counted;
We have boasted our belief in you but disobeyed your
    will:
We have been self-confident, taken our eyes off you
    and denied you.

We pray therefore for courage to come out from our
    churches into your world,
We pray for the perseverance to do your will even
    when this is the hardest way,
We pray for the strength to speak out for the gospel
    and to live our lives accordingly,

We pray for obedience even when it may seem dull or
    irrelevant.
This we pray that we may see your glory in our lives,
    not through our own efforts but through your love
    for your creation.
Through Jesus Christ our Lord. Amen.

(b) Confession

51.   Father, source of all power, we confess that we do not
always use the powers you have given us as you intend.
Sometimes we are afraid of the power we wield, and so
we do not use it at all: at other times we are careless in
our use of it and harm others; at yet other times we
deliberately misuse it to achieve our own selfish ends.
We confess our misuse of our God-given powers. And
ask for your grace to use them properly in future.
Amen.

52.   Gracious Lord, we bring before you our personal failures in our daily work. We have been poor stewards of
your gifts, we have not given you the glory, nor laboured
in your love. We confess too the faults of our industrial
society; continuing injustice, lack of harmony, the inability and, worse, the unwillingness, to seek the paths
of reconciliation. Have mercy upon us and grant that, as
the workshop of Nazareth was blessed through the
labour of the Christ, so the workshops of this land may
be enriched through the work of those who call him
'Lord'. In His name. Amen.

53.   Lord of the Universe, we praise you for your creation,
for the wonder of space, the beauty of the world, and the
value of the earth's resources. We praise you for the
many different skills of hand and brain.
We recognise that we often spoil these gifts by our
selfishness, and because we are sometimes distrustful
and destructive.

Forgive us we pray. Help us to use all that you give to us
for the good of all people.
Through Jesus Christ our Lord. Amen.

54. Most merciful and holy Father, we confess that we are a
sinful people. We have failed to love you and your
creation. We love in order to be loved; we serve for
recognition; we allow ourselves to be separated from
you. We are too concerned with prestige, with being
right, with being busy. We have refused to live in the
uncertainty that faith requires. We fear to stand before
the world for your sake. Indeed, our sin is much worse
because we claim to be doing your work. We have talked
much but done little. O Lord, we stand before you
guilty. Have mercy upon us, for Jesus Christ's sake.
Amen.

55. God, our Father, we admit to you that we have failed to
be the men and women you meant us to be.
When duty has called we have shirked it, and we have
defended ourselves with excuses which did not convince
us, let alone deceive you.
We are sorry for our failure, which has hurt ourselves as
well as others, and we resolve to put right what can be
put right. And as for those mistakes which cannot be
changed and constantly accuse us, we surrender them to
you. Save us from being haunted by them.
Release us from their burden, so that we can step into
the future unafraid, knowing that, even if we fail, failure
does not put us out of reach of your help, which comes to
us through Jesus Christ our Lord. Amen.

(c) Commitment

56. We dedicate to you, O God, the industries of our
country that all of us who work therein, whether by hand
or brain, may serve to your glory and the good of others:
through Jesus Christ our Lord. Amen.

57. We dedicate to you, O God, the industries and agriculture of our land, especially those of this town and district, that all who work therein may serve to your glory and the good of their fellow-men; through Jesus Christ our Lord. Amen.

58. O Lord, we know that this world is yours. We know that we can only make sense of the world as we obey your will within it; so we come afresh to dedicate ourselves; the work in which we are involved every day; and our hopes for the future, through Jesus Christ our Lord. Amen.

59. Father of all, we humbly offer you the service of our lives. Refresh us when we are tired. Grant us the discipline to live simply, that others may simply live. Take our lives, O Lord, and make us instruments of your will, ministers in your service and builders of your Kingdom. Give us grace to serve the needs of others, to persevere in truth and persist in prayer, and live with resolute goodwill, so that our work may be begun, continued and ended in you. Through Jesus Christ our Lord. Amen.

60. We commit our future work to you, O Lord, so that you may make us instruments of your grace, ministers in your service, and creators in your Kingdom.
We also commit ourselves to serve the needs of others, to persevere in truth, to persist in prayer and good works and at all times to seek your goodwill, so that daily work, begun, continued and ended in you may be done to your praise and glory. Amen.

61. Heavenly Father, whose Blessed Son Jesus Christ has shown us that the secret of happiness is a heart set free from selfish desires, help us all to look not only on our own things, but also on the things of others and inspire in us such fair-dealing and fellow-feeling as may show forth our brotherhood with you. Through the same Jesus Christ our Lord. Amen.

62. O Christ, the Master Carpenter, who at the last through wood and nails purchased man's whole salvation, wield well your tools in the workshop of your world, so that we who come rough-hewn to your bench may here be fashioned to a truer beauty of your hand. We ask it for your own Name's sake. Amen.

63. O Jesus Christ, Master Carpenter, you who so loved the world that you became one with us in your birth, life and death, accept, we beseech you, the offering and dedication of ourselves as your fellow workers for the salvation of your world. Wield all your tools within the workshop of our offices and factories, our cities and communities, that we may together with our fellow men be changed into your likeness and may establish your Kingdom on earth. Amen.

64. Gracious God, we praise you for what you have given and for what you have promised us. You have led us to identify with the human struggle. You have fed us with your word and renewed us for your work. Now we give ourselves to you; and ask that our daily work may be part of the life of your Kingdom, and that our love may be your love reaching out into the life of the world. Amen.

65. O God of all power and all love, you have created us to depend on one another. Make us aware of our reliance on the work and integrity of our fellows. Make us sensitive to their needs and their requirements of us, and by your grace enable us to serve them faithfully and wisely. Father we commit our lives to your service, through Jesus Christ our Lord. Amen.

(d) Thanksgiving

66. Almighty God, we praise you for all your gifts to us in creation. We acknowledge the skills with which we have been endowed, the materials available for our use and the opportunities to meet the needs of others. We thank you for what British industry and commerce has achieved, for its contribution to our lives and the relief of need. We offer ourselves for your service, through Jesus Christ our Lord. Amen.

67. May our gratitude to you, Almighty God, be plain in all that we do. May we be filled with an enduring sense of thankfulness for the wealth and variety of the world, for the ability of man and for the hopes instilled in us. Allow us to return all these gifts to you with love and praise and in humility derived from knowing you to be Alpha and Omega, the Creator and the End. We praise your name and your power above all else. Amen.

68. Almighty God, Creator and Lord of all things, we thank you for the vast resources of the earth and the sea, and for the hidden forces of nature now brought within our control by scientific discovery.
We thank you again for the different abilities and skills which you have given us and which we use in daily work.
Help us to use all your gifts wisely and faithfully for the benefit of mankind, that all may rejoice in your goodness. Through Jesus Christ our Lord. Amen.

69. Let us thank God that he maintains this world and directs it towards the future. For the courage of many people in faith and love, we thank him: that children are born and the dead are mourned, that there is love between man and woman and friendship across all borders. We thank him for the energy and dedication with which people are working in factories, offices and universities, in studios and laboratories towards free and truly human relations. And we thank him for the promise that justice and righteousness and truth will be stronger than injustice and destruction everywhere on earth, in this place and in ourselves. Amen.

70. O God, the Creator of all things, we thank you for making man in your own likeness, for his wisdom to devise and skill to accomplish all kinds of work, for enabling him to share in the continuing work of your Creation. We rejoice in the ability to explore the secrets of nature, in the new discoveries and opportunities of this age, through which human life may be enriched and the cause of your Kingdom be advanced. Through Jesus Christ. Amen.

71. We thank you, God, for all the variety of the human race.
We thank you for our dependence on other people's skill, labour and love.
We are glad that our experience is enriched by men and women from every walk of life, of every colour, language and belief.
We praise you for the development and unfolding of human character.
Most of all we thank you that Jesus lived a human life, as our example, our teacher and our Saviour.
May we learn the most valuable lessons from life, and become useful servants of our fellow men. Amen.

72. We give thanks for the daily miracle by which we are fed:
for the heat of the sun
for the fertile earth
for changing seasons
for the work of men and women in the open air, and in factories
for traffic and transport by day and by night, by land, sea and air
for all in this country and around the world, on whose faithful work we depend for food, clothing and housing. Amen.

73. Father, for all the good gifts of the earth, for food and drink,

for bread and milk, flowers and vegetables,
for the earth's minerals and animals,
for the work of farmers at home and abroad,
for those who work on allotments and in gardens
we want to say 'Thank you, Lord'.
Help us to make the most of these gifts to help those
    who have less than we have and to improve poor
    lands;
For Jesus Christ's sake. Amen.

74. Father,
for families, for our neighbours, for friends old and
    new,
for our own lives, and the new opportunities this city
    presents,
for all we learn from each other and the life of Jesus
    Christ,
We want to say 'Thank you, Lord'.

Help us to break down barriers and misunderstanding,
to forgive, to care and to grow together:
For Jesus Christ's sake. Amen.

75. Father,
for the work of industries that build houses and give
    people homes,
for the industries that supply us with the goods we need
    to live,
for the industries that help to fight illness and care for
    people,
for the industries that service all our needs,
We want to say 'Thank you, Lord'.

Help us to build a society worth living in,
help us to build bridges of love and friendship with
    those with whom we work,
help us to show your love.
For Jesus Christ's sake. Amen.

LITANIES

(a) Confession
(b) Creed
(c) Intercessions
(d) Thanksgiving

LITANIES

(a) Confession

76. Being assured of your power to relieve sin, we bring before you, Lord, all the failures of daily work. We have fallen short of your demands upon us, we have not given you the Glory nor worked in your love.
Good Lord forgive us – *Forgive us, Lord.*

We confess the faults of the industrial society in which we work, the inequalities and injustices of all the systems and the difficulties experienced in changing them. We especially regret the waste of human resources through unemployment and the fear and reality of redundancy.
Good Lord forgive us – *Forgive us, Lord.*

We seek forgiveness for all broken relationships, disputes and strikes. There have been differences, a lack of harmony and chances of reconciliation missed. We have not contributed enough to the spirit of co-operation.
Good Lord forgive us – *Forgive us, Lord.*

We have wasted and misused the resources of the earth and often absorbed more than our fair share of them. We have not made the best use of the time and skill you have given us. We fear for the consequences of our actions that we pass on to future generations.
Good Lord forgive us – *Forgive us, Lord.*

We have not met the needs of the hungry and impoverished of the world. We have been unable to meet the demands of those without work, nor lay properly the foundations for future prosperity and a fair distribution of your wealth.
Good Lord forgive us – *Forgive us, Lord.*

77. Lord forgive us our sins, as we forgive those who sin
against us . . .

Lord I have been hurt,
Perhaps not much, but enough for me,
Enough to be bruised and offended and touchy,
Enough to make me cover up my hurt with patience,
or with courage and smiles and briskness,
or with dignity, contempt and self-righteousness
or with sulks and self defence.
LORD SET ME FREE TO FORGIVE.

I tell myself there is nothing to forgive but I nurse my
grudges.
LORD SET ME FREE.

I try to forgive but I nurse my grudges.
LORD SET ME FREE.

I pretend to forgive but I nurse my grudges.
LORD SET ME FREE.

I think I have forgiven but I still nurse my grudges.
LORD SET ME FREE.

Lord, my grudges are real
Don't let me brush them aside; uncover them,
That I may forgive, let me see them.

Then set me free
to forgive my family and friends
to forgive the people where I work
to forgive the people in power
to forgive my enemy
to forgive my neighbour
to forgive myself.
LORD SET ME FREE TO FORGIVE
AND BE FORGIVEN THROUGH
JESUS CHRIST, MY SALVATION.
AMEN.

78. Let us celebrate Christ, and examine ourselves in his presence;
Christ is patient – always ready to listen, always ready to talk:
Lord, teach us to be patient.
Christ is at home everywhere, with everyone, including the lepers of society:
Lord, help us to be open to all.
Christ is relentless with those who oppress others:
Lord, make us instruments of your justice.
Christ sees us as we are – and gives us new names:
Lord, help us to see ourselves and others as you do.
Christ is the incarnation of love – he gives himself:
Lord, help us to give ourselves.
Christ forgives those who forgive:
Lord, help us to forgive.
Christ suffers and dies for the world:
Lord, help us to be living sacrifices for you.

79. Let us remember how God's loving purposes are thwarted by our misuse of his gifts and by our neglect of his commands; and let us ask his forgiveness.
The HATRED which divides nation from nation, race from race, class from class,
Father, forgive.
The COVETOUS desires of men and nations to possess what is not their own,
Father, forgive.
The GREED which exploits the labours of men, and lays waste the earth,
Father, forgive.
Our ENVY of the welfare and happiness of others,
Father, forgive.
Our INDIFFERENCE to the plight of the homeless and the refugee,
Father, forgive.
The LUST which uses for ignoble ends the bodies of men and women,
Father, forgive.

The PRIDE which leads us to trust in ourselves, and not in God,

> *Father, forgive.*

80. It is the will of God that men should deal justly with one another, and live in fellowship and love.
Our lack of brotherhood, our selfishness in dealings with one another:

> *O Lord, forgive.*

It is the will of God that men should support the weak and care for the aged, protect the young, and strengthen the tempted.
Our unconcern for others:

> *O Lord, forgive.*

It is the will of God that men should find happiness and fulfilment in their work, peace in their homes, and renewed strength in their recreation.
Our lack of purpose, our feeble sense of duty, and our feverish search for excitement:

> *O Lord, forgive.*

It is the will of God that men should follow Christ, in every moment of every day.
Our failure to acknowledge you as the Lord of all life, and our lack of courage in upholding the right:

> *O Lord, forgive.*

81. O God of truth, for lies, deceit and fraud, in commerce and in advertising, in politics and journalism, in all that is done by the written and spoken word to cajole and deceive for religious or secular ends;
We ask for your forgiveness.

O God who was made man, for the sins of men against men: in cruelty and terror, in blockade and war, in greedy and selfish neglect of the helpless, in the ruthless cutting of family ties;
We ask for your forgiveness.

O God of our salvation, for the abuse of power and the contempt of misery, for the callous disregard of the old and of orphans, of all who cannot and do not find the love and care that they need;
We ask for your forgiveness.

O God of justice, for the oppression of minorities and the persecution of those who dissent from the dominant group for political, religious, or social reasons, for our own blindness, our vested interests, and for our unwillingness to learn from others;
We ask for your forgiveness.

O God of mercy, for our ingratitude, for all our failures in imagination where the needs of others are concerned, for our misuse of material resources, for the wrong motives of our good deeds;
We ask for your forgiveness.

O God of peace, for our quarrels and wars, for all the divisions and hatreds between Christian men and women, for broken homes and marriages where love has gone, for lost friendships;
We ask for your forgiveness.

Lord in your mercy, grant that we may receive, now, forgiveness through faith in the gospel. In the Name of Jesus. Amen.

(b) Creed

82. Do you believe in God?
We believe in One God, Father Almighty, Maker of heaven and earth,
Source of man's skills, Provider of earth's riches.
In God who is love, and judge of all, who claims our service and worship, longs for our help in creation, to fulfil his purpose on earth.

Do you believe in Jesus Christ?
We believe in Jesus Christ, the only begotten Son of God,
The Light of the World,
The Lord of all life, The man for others.
Our fellow-worker for good, our Redeemer, neighbour
and friend,
With the power to make all things new.

Do you believe in the Holy Spirit?
We believe in the Holy Spirit, God's inspiration to man,
Revealer of the Truth, the Giver and Director of life, the
promoter of Peace and Patience, our Comforter in times
of trouble, and supplier of vision and hope. Amen.

83. Do you believe in God?
I believe in God the Father, Maker of the Universe. He
gives unity and order to all created things. He gives us the
resources of the earth to sustain human life. He enables us
to share in the continuing work of creation with our vision
and our skill.

Do you believe in Jesus Christ?
I believe in Jesus Christ, the Son of God. He worked as a
carpenter and gave value to all human labour. He cared
for people at their point of need. He died because of
human hatred and jealousy. He rose to new life and is
alive today.

Do you believe in the Holy Spirit?
I believe in the Holy Spirit. He makes Jesus Christ real to
us. He inspires us to follow the pattern of Jesus' life. He
helps us through the tension and uncertainty of our daily
work. He gives us hope for the future along with other
Christians.

(c) Intercessions

84. We pray for the nations of the world;
   for our own country;

  for the world of industry and commerce;
  for peace and reconciliation between men.
Lord, in your mercy
Hear our prayer.

We pray for society;
  for those who work and maintain the fabric of our
  community;
  for the unemployed, the under-employed and the
  overworked;
  for those with responsibility for education, training
  and research;
  for those who work in the mass media.
Lord, in your mercy
Hear our prayer.

We pray for the Church;
  for the reconciling ministry of this Church;
  for the Industrial Mission Teams;
  for the work of industrial chaplains;
  for all Christians in their place of work.
Lord, in your mercy
Hear our prayer.

85. For the riches of your creation, giving us the materials of
the earth;
     We thank you, Lord.
For the labour of our hands and minds, developing
invention and skill;
     We thank you, Lord.
For industry and commerce, providing work and wealth
and goods for the world;
     We thank you, Lord.
For all who work in industry and commerce that in
giving service they may find reward;
     Hear our prayer.
For those in Management and the Trade Unions, that
mutual respect and good relations always be main-
tained;
     Hear our prayer.

For the unemployed and the handicapped, that they may not lose hope, and may find a positive role in life;
>*Hear our prayer.*

For young people in industry and commerce, and those who educate and train them, that they may find promise and aspiration fulfilled;
>*Hear our prayer.*

Lord the Creator, whose great goodness has provided for our needs; help us so to use, develop and preserve the resources of the earth that, through our industry, the needs of many may be fulfilled, the dignity of man enhanced, and our people live in true prosperity and peace. Through Jesus Christ our Lord. *Amen.*

86. Let us pray for all who are involved in mission in industry, and that all men and women will increasingly work together for the good of all and for the welfare of the community.
>Lord in your mercy
>*Hear our prayer.*

That the rich resources of the earth will be used to do away with deprivation and inequality, and bring security and happiness to all people.
>Lord in your mercy
>*Hear our prayer.*

That people at work will find dignity and fulfilment in developing their own creativity and the sharing in a wider responsibility for wealth and power.
>Lord in your mercy
>*Hear our prayer.*

That God will accept the offering of the world of commerce and industry and help us to work with him, through Jesus Christ our Lord. *Amen.*

87. O God the Father, Creator of all things:
>HAVE MERCY UPON US.

O God the Son, Redeemer of the world:
>HAVE MERCY UPON US.

O God the Holy Spirit, Giver of life:

HAVE MERCY UPON US.

O Holy, blessed and glorious Trinity, three Persons and one God:

HAVE MERCY UPON US.

From envy, avarice and status-seeking, from covetousness which is idolatory; from wanting more than our fair share:

GOOD LORD, DELIVER US.

From ruthlessness in making money, and from irresponsibility in spending it:

GOOD LORD, DELIVER US.

From unwillingness to know the cost to others of our own standard of living:

GOOD LORD, DELIVER US.

From unwillingness to face the cost to ourselves of meeting the needs of others:

GOOD LORD, DELIVER US.

For financiers and politicians, industrialists and trade unionists, and all who wield economic power; that they may have grace, wisdom and compassion:

LORD, HEAR OUR PRAYER.

For the bewildered and inadequate who can't cope with a budget or with filling in forms or with the pressures of modern life:

LORD, HEAR OUR PRAYER.

For the victims of inflation, old age pensioners, people on small fixed incomes, and all who are robbed of their savings:

LORD, HEAR OUR PRAYER.

For those who cannot find jobs, or homes they can afford, for human beings made redundant by 'increased productivity' or mergers:

LORD, HEAR OUR PRAYER.

For the increase of the fruits of the earth and that all men may enjoy them:

LORD, HEAR OUR PRAYER.

Lord, when we are deciding how to make money, how to steward it, and what to do with it,

Help us to look hard at our motives and our presuppositions and our aims – honestly – in your sight.

O Lord Jesus Christ, who for our sakes became poor, grant us grace to forsake all covetous desires and inordinate love of riches, and to seek first the Kingdom of God and his righteousness. Through Jesus Christ, our Lord:

AMEN.

88. First Person: We bless God for his creation, for making men and women in his own image, and for his never-failing love for us all: let us pray for his world, that it may more perfectly reflect his glory, and be re-created in Jesus Christ.

Second person: We pray for all nations to whom you have given power and wealth. May they use your gifts for the good of mankind, that all may share the riches of your world. We pray for our country and for all who bear the burdens of responsibility, that they may lead the nation in the ways of justice and peace; and we pray also for our own communities that we may be led away from hatred and greed so as to love and honour everyone.

First Person: We pray for all who produce food. May the gifts of the earth be neither selfishly hoarded nor foolishly squandered, but used to satisfy the needs of all.

Second Person: We pray for all who work in industry and commerce. Inspire us all with the spirit of goodwill, that all human relations and every place of work may embody your love and your justice.

First Person: We pray for the unemployed and all whose jobs are insecure. Give to them and us the assurance of their worth as your children: and enable us so to order society that all may use their gifts for the common good.

Second Person: We pray for all who seek justice: that together we may overcome hatred with love, evil with goodness, and falsehood with truth. May people of different races respect each other. Forgive your Church that men and women have not seen in it the hope of a new order; and grant that through it the kingdoms of this world may be transformed into the Kingdom of Heaven. Through Christ our Lord. *Amen*.

89. Let us pray that all men may learn to seek first the Kingdom of God and his righteousness, caring for justice more than for gain, and for fellowship between men more than for the domination of others.
Lord hear our prayer.
Let us pray that all may have the courage and the energy to think for themselves strongly and clearly, and to seek for the truth and follow it whatever the cost.
Lord hear our prayer.
Let us pray for deliverance from prejudice and for a desire to appreciate what is just and true in the opinions of those who differ from us.
Lord hear our prayer.
Let us pray for those who bear the heavy responsibility of Government in the nations of the world. As in duty

bound we pray for Elizabeth our Queen and all who bear office under her, in national Government and in the life of this place.

Lord hear our prayer.

Let us pray for the troubled parts of the world especially where there is violence and oppression, the clash of race, and grave disparity between those who are affluent and those who are deprived.

Lord hear our prayer.

Let us pray for all as they go about their daily work, thanking God for the many skills of hand and brain. Let us pray that our education shall prepare all citizens more adequately, not only for their work but also for their leisure.

Lord hear our prayer.

Let us pray most particularly this day for those engaged in the industrial and commercial life of this country that wages may be fair, organisation efficient and marketing honest.

Lord hear our prayer.

Let us pray that we may all have a concern for each other at work, for enlightened and enterprising management, for well organised and responsible trade unions, for imaginative and well conceived industrial relations.

Lord hear our prayer.

Let us pray that God will grant peace in our time both between nations and within nations and give us abundantly of his Holy Spirit, whose fruits are love and joy and peace. Let us pray that we may use his gifts to enrich life and not to destroy it.

Lord hear our prayer. Amen.

90.   We bring before you, O God, our desires and our hopes;

That management in industry may be ordered and strengthened in justice and truth;

That those employed in industry may work together in harmony;

That from true service each may gain due and proper
  reward;
HEAR US, O LORD.

That our industry may serve the common good;
That it may bring a fuller life to all the peoples of the
  world;
That in its products and power it may bless, protect and
  delight, but not destroy;
HEAR US, O LORD.

That your spirit may guide all who lead in industry;
  employers and owners, works committees and trade
  unions, managers, foremen and shop stewards;
That your spirit may lead all research workers and
  scientists;
HEAR US, O LORD.

That you protect men and women in the perils and
  dangers of their work;
That all young workers may be responsibly trained and
  cared for in body, mind and character;
That you bless all welfare work, ambulance work, and
  provision for the elderly;
That you bless all those who are unemployed and guide
  those responsible for finding useful work for them to
  do;
HEAR US, O LORD.

Teach us, O Lord, to engage with faith and zeal in
  mission, for the mission is yours, and by your
  commission you can make it ours. Strengthen and
  uphold all who are called to work in Industrial
  Mission. May we all by our life and words make
  known your Christ to the waiting world.
AMEN.

91. Let us remember before God the men whose lives are
  formed and moulded by the industries of our land.

Remembering
those whose work demands sheer hard physical toil;
those who work before the heat of the furnace or
    amidst the noise of machinery;
those who work on the heights of new buildings;
those who work in the depths of the mines;
those whose work is monotonous or pointless;
those who continue working in the face of injustice and
    oppression;
those who fear redundancy and are too old to begin
    again.
O Lord, fill us with understanding, and teach us to care.

Remembering also
those who have responsibility for directing the work of
    others;
those who feel lonely at the top, or who are baffled by
    the problems of finding work for their fellow men;
those who are responsible for the moral decisions of
    how man's new-found powers are to be used;
those who are faced daily with decisions which conflict
    with conscience.
O Lord, fill us with understanding, and teach us to care.

Remembering also leaders of Trade Unions and
    Management organisations in their search for justice
    and fair dealing.
Remembering those responsible for the training of the
    young and the retraining of those who require to
    learn new skills.
And remembering the work of the Church in
    Industry – the witness of all faithful Christians, in
    personal service – in group loyalty and brotherhood.
    And the work of the Chaplains who support them.
O Lord, fill us with understanding, and teach us to care.

O Lord God who has given it into the hands of man in
this generation so to master the forces of your creation,
that he may have wealth and power; help us also to

master our common life in Christ's name, that all the
work of men being first offered to you may bring
blessing to those that labour, and happiness to the
whole community.

Through Jesus Christ our Lord. *Amen.*

92. We pray for the Church of Jesus Christ;
for a renewal of its faith and sense of mission through
a new experience of the Living Lord in the midst of his
people, uniting us through his challenge to love one
another and accept one another.
May the Church become a community of love and
compassion, of healing and of hope, in the midst of a
world of need.
Lord in your mercy
Hear our prayer.

We pray for this community,
for its officers and elected representatives, magis-
trates, police and social workers, all who have influence and authority, and make decisions that affect
the lives of their fellows.
Particularly we pray for those who hold together community life in shops and offices, schools and churches
and clinics, in homes and clubs and on the streets.
Hear us as we name the people who carry a heavy
burden on their hearts in this community.
Lord in your mercy
Hear our prayer.

We pray for all industrialists and employers,
coping with the difficulties of the present financial
recession, and faced with decisions that affect the
lives of so many.
Help them to see each employee as a person and not just
a number, and to show justice and integrity in their
management, concerned for efficiency and the proper

use of investment, but also for the good of the indus-
try and the community.
Lord in your mercy
Hear our prayer.

We pray for all Trade Unionists, and particularly their
leaders;
that they may exercise their influence wisely and
responsibly, for the good and well-being of their
members but also the industry and the community.
Lord in your mercy
Hear our prayer.

We pray for those whose work is dull and monotonous;
for those whose work is dangerous, or threatens their
family life by difficult hours or enforced absence for
long periods.
Above all we pray for those who cannot find work and
for whom redundancy or unemployment undermines
their confidence in themselves, and reduces life to dull
monotony.
Help us in our society to know the privilege of work, and
to be ready to share its benefits more widely, that all
may find a purpose in their lives.
Lord in your mercy
*Accept our prayers for the sake of your Son our Saviour
Jesus Christ.*
Amen.

93. Let us remember that the first recorded command of
God to man was that he was to work . . .
Let us ask God's forgiveness for the times when we
have viewed our own work only as a means of getting
money rather than a gift of God . . .
Lord in your Mercy – HEAR OUR PRAYER.

Let us pray for all employers of labour that they may
never forget that the happiness of other people depends
so much on them.

Let us pray for the members of this congregation who are employers that they may live out, at their works, the truths they learn and agree to here . . .

Lord in your Mercy – HEAR OUR PRAYER.

Let us pray for all who are employed by others that they may delight to give of their best in their work . . .

Let us pray that all of us who are members of the Church may seek above all to please God through our work . . .

Lord in your Mercy – HEAR OUR PRAYER.

Let us pray for the Trades Union Movement thanking God for all that has been achieved in getting better conditions and fairer wages for workers . . .

Let us pray for Trades Union Officers, especially all leaders of the various unions together with shop stewards, that they may exercise their powers responsibly and with integrity and humility . . .

Lord in your Mercy – HEAR OUR PRAYER.

Let us pray for the Employers' Federations, for all Economists and the Government and its Ministers, that at this time when so much divides us as a nation and when industry is so threatened, they may know how God would have them direct our affairs in justice and in peace . . .

Lord in your Mercy – HEAR OUR PRAYER.

Let us pray for those with whom we are linked through work, our colleagues at work, those who serve us day by day – the newsboy, the postman, the milkman, the dustman, the shop assistant and all who labour on our behalf – that we may treat them as we would treat Christ . . .

Lord in your Mercy – HEAR OUR PRAYER.

Let us pray for those whose work is without creative skill, for those whose work takes them away from home, for those whose work brings them into situations where they are greatly tempted and for all whose work is dangerous . . .

Lord in your Mercy – HEAR OUR PRAYER.

Let us pray for those who cannot work, for those who cannot find employment, for those who are looked down on at work because of their colour or their political attitudes, for those who are disabled and those who are retired . . .

Lord in your Mercy – HEAR OUR PRAYER.

O Jesus, Master Carpenter of Nazareth, who on the cross through wood and nails didst work man's whole salvation; wield well thy tools in this workshop, that we who come to thee rough-hewn may, by Thy hand, be fashioned to a truer beauty and a greater usefulness . . .

Lord in your Mercy – HEAR OUR PRAYER.

94. Let us pray
for all employers and employers' associations that they may never forget how much the well-being of others depends on them;
for members of this congregation who are employers that they may live out daily the truths they learn and consent to within Christ's Church.

Lord, in your mercy . . . *Hear our prayer.*

Let us pray
for all who are employed by others that they may delight to give of their best in their work;
for all who follow Christ that they may seek above all to please him through their work.

Lord, in your mercy . . . *Hear our prayer.*

Let us pray
for the Trades Union Movement, thanking God for what it has achieved in improving the wages and working conditions of workers;

for the leaders of the various unions, together with shop-stewards and members, that they may exercise their power responsibly and with integrity and concern for the common good.

    Lord, in your mercy . . . *Hear our prayer*.

Let us pray
for the Government and all members of Parliament that, at this time, when so much divides us as a nation and when industry is so threatened, they may know how God would have them direct our affairs in justice and peace.

    Lord, in your mercy . . . *Hear our prayer*.

Let us pray
for those with whom we are linked through work, for those who serve us day by day – the newsboy, the postman, the milkman, dustman, shop assistant and all who labour on our behalf – that we may treat them as we would treat the Christ, who came amongst us as one who served.

    Lord, in your mercy . . . *Hear our prayer*.

Let us pray
for those whose work lacks creative fulfilment;
for those whose work takes them away from home;
for those whose work brings great temptation;
for all whose work is dangerous.

    Lord, in your mercy . . . *Hear our prayer*

Let us pray
for those who cannot find work, for some who will not work, those looked down on at work because of colour, political or religious beliefs, for the disabled and for those who are retired.

    Lord, in your mercy . . . *Hear our prayer*.

95. Father, whose Son said that his kingdom was not of this world, you have put us into our world, help us to know how to pray for it. We are puzzled and concerned for all the conflicts and challenges that surround us in our everyday lives, and today we hold in your presence the concerns of our working environment in these times of change.

We pray for the proper use of our material resources; for wisdom in the management of mineral deposits; for wisdom in the worldwide development of agriculture; for the ecological balance between the need for food and the need to maintain the natural balance of forests, water and cultivated land; for balance in the harvesting of animals and fish; for the need to develop an environment in which all the peoples of the world may be enabled to live and grow as their, and our economies alter, often with alarming speed.

Lord, we pray for your guidance, may we act in your spirit.

We pray for all those in positions of power who are trying to plan ahead for the correct use of technology and manpower; for those who work in co-operation with other governments; for those who advise the multi-national consortiums; for those employed in the EEC; for all who contribute to vast organisations; for any who feel that their contribution is so small that it makes no difference how they act.

Lord, we pray for your guidance, may we act in your spirit.

We pray for those in this country whom we have chosen for positions of leadership: politicians, heads of department, managers, trades union leaders, shop stewards, negotiators, newspaper editors, television and radio reporters, the clergy, leaders of pressure groups and anyone who is in a position to make decisions affecting other people's lives. We may be one of those and we know that we need your help. Give us humility to wait patiently for your will, and courage to play our full part in whatever action is necessary.

Lord, we pray for your guidance, may we act in your spirit.

We pray for all who enjoy their work. We thank you for the satisfaction it brings, for the physical and mental weariness that can be refreshed by sleep or relaxation, when we have finished;
for all who travel to work, or during work, for all the people they meet, for all the opportunities for communication in gesture, touch or word;
for all who work alone, quietly, in communion with nature or their home surroundings;
for those who work amid noise, bustle and activity all around.

Lord, we pray for your guidance, may we act in your spirit.

We pray for those who feel threatened by the rate of change around them; for those who may be relieved of dull boring work, but who see no prospect of employment; for those trying to find the courage or the money to retrain, or to move to another area where there is work; for men and women who are worried about their families and their standard of living; for all of those who think it will never happen to them and who are indifferent to the needs of others as long as they themselves feel secure; for all who find no one to turn to for help; for all who do care, who do pray and who are representing your spirit of growth in the spiral of change.

Lord, we pray for your guidance, may we act in your spirit.

We pray for ourselves, and for our own work, or lack of it; for our friends or colleagues who have too much work or too little; for those who hide in their work and leave no time for other gifts of family or leisure; for those who do not know how to use the leisure they have, or who dread retirement and having time on their hands.

We pray that we may each look afresh at the place of work and of leisure in our own lives and that we may contribute through prayer, discussion and action to the changing processes that involve us all.

Lord, we pray for guidance, may we act in your spirit.

(d) Thanksgiving

96. O Lord God Almighty, we offer you thanks for the chance to work, for the opportunity to create and add value, to improve the quality of life and to work towards the building of your Kingdom.
O Lord, accept our thanks – *Accept our heartfelt thanks.*

We are thankful for the provision of human skill and natural resource, for the new discoveries and developments, and for the use of them to which man is privileged.
O Lord, accept our thanks – *Accept our heartfelt thanks.*

We are grateful for previous generations who laid the foundations of our society, for the facilities that educate and train us for the future, and for those who care for our present welfare.
O Lord, accept our thanks – *Accept our heartfelt thanks.*

We have relished the chance to deepen relationships with colleagues at work, to welcome new-comers, to be open and to care for those in need.

O Lord, accept our thanks – *Accept our heartfelt thanks.*

We offer you Lord, ourselves and our work. Please accept it as a token of our gratitude to you, for all your goodness to us, and in the hope that it has helped to build your Kingdom on earth, through Jesus Christ our Lord. *Amen.*

97. We give thanks to God the Father, Maker of the Universe,
> for the unity and order of created things;
> for the resources of the earth;
> for the gift of human life;
> for our share in the continuing work of creation;
> for creative vision and inventive skill;
> for industry and commerce.

Let us bless the Lord:
> *Thanks be to God.*

We give thanks to God in Jesus Christ,
> for his obedience fulfilled on the cross;
> for his bearing of the sin of the world;
> for his victory over evil and death;
> for his care for people;
> for the value he gave to human labour;
> for all our opportunities of work and leisure.

Let us bless the Lord:
> *Thanks be to God.*

We give thanks to God, the Holy Spirit,
> for his continuing presence and power in the world;
> for the harvest of the Spirit in the lives of men –
> for love, joy, peace, patience, kindness, goodness, faithfulness, gentleness and self-control;
> for the strength of the Spirit which enables and inspires us to persevere through troubles and difficulties.

Let us bless the Lord:
> *Thanks be to God.*

98.   For our own calling to share in the creating work of
        God.
        Praise the Lord.
        The Lord's name be praised.

For the earth giving of her bounty to meet the needs of
    man.
For the skills and techniques men have devised to help
    them.
For the patient labour of the beasts and their
    friendship.
    Praise the Lord.
    The Lord's name be praised.

For all the resources hidden deep in the earth or won
    from the sea.
For the strength and speed of machines.
For the plenty and comfort which can be made
    available to man.
    Praise the Lord.
    The Lord's name be praised.

For satisfaction in work well done, and for loyalty and
    friendship in the doing of it.
For the joy we can find in the contentment and
    happiness of our homes and families, of our country
    and of mankind.
For the knowledge that we may meet with God in the
    common ways of life and in the service of our
    fellow-men.
    Praise the Lord.
    The Lord's name be praised.

99.   O God our Father, we praise and thank you because we
see you are creator of this universe.
*We acknowledge you and praise you as Lord of all
creation.*

We praise and thank you because we see you at work, as

men and women put to good use the raw material of creation; experiment, plant and build; manufacture; produce and use all that is entrusted to us.
We acknowledge you and praise you as the Lord of industry and commerce, science and technology.

We praise and thank you because we see you co-operating with men in their work, seeking to make things of true value, reconciling differences between management and workers, and bringing peace to the world of industry.
We acknowledge you and praise you as the Lord of reconciliation.

We praise you and thank you because we see you leading people to discover the meaning and purpose of life.
We acknowledge you as the Lord of truth and life.

We praise you and thank you because we see condemned on the Cross on which Jesus was killed, selfishness, pride, the avoidance of responsibility, hardheartedness and cowardice; and see exalted as the hope of all, the love that seeks to save and be spent in the service of others, the love that sacrifices, the love that unites and the love that conquers.
We acknowledge and praise you as the source and Lord of Love.

100. Let us give thanks to God for all the good things of life. Let us give thanks for the world in which we live, and the universe beyond it.
For these and all good things we give thanks.

Let us give thanks for those who throughout the ages have pioneered along new paths of thought and knowledge, opening the minds of men to new adventures of truth.
For these and all good things we give thanks.

Let us give thanks for the heritage of our common life; for wise government and good laws; for education and art, science and technology, and all their benefits to us.
For these and all good things we give thanks.

Let us give thanks for the comforts and pleasures of life, for our homes and our friends; for the goodwill and companionship of men; for the help, sympathy and advice of those who are wiser than ourselves.
For these and all good things we give thanks.

Let us give thanks for this community, for what we owe to industry and all who have helped to build it up.
For these and all good things we give thanks.

Let us give thanks for those on whose labour we depend for the necessities of life, all those engaged with us in industry, whether manufacturing goods or providing services, and in commerce.
For all on whom we depend, we give thanks.

Let us give thanks for all those scientists and doctors whose researches and devoted work have bettered the health of mankind, and those who today in hospitals and laboratories fight to free men from slavery to disease.
For all on whom we depend for health, we give thanks.

Let us give thanks for those who have helped to lighten the load of drudgery at work and at home, and who have enriched the possibilities of our leisure time.
For all on whom we depend for enjoyment, we give thanks.

Let us give thanks for men and women of all ages who have done anything in any way to improve the quality of human life.
For all good things and people, we give thanks.

READINGS: BIBLICAL

(a) Readings in biblical order
(b) Readings in subject order

READINGS: BIBLICAL

(a) Readings in biblical order

The following section lists references to biblical readings with a summary of their content only, rather than the full Bible texts themselves.

(i) Old Testament

101. GENESIS 1:1–end
Creation, the world and its resources are ordered according to God's will.

102. GENESIS 1:26–31a
The destiny of man. God grants man control over his creation.

103. GENESIS 4:3–9
Man spoils God's creation through greed and jealousy.

104. EXODUS 1:8–14, 3:1–9
God sees and understands oppression; suffering through work is condemned by God.

105. EXODUS 18:13–23
The delegation of power is a right use of authority, keeping control of power by one person is an abuse.

106. EXODUS 31:1–11
The dedication of skilled work. All work is to the glorification of God as creator.

107. EXODUS 35:30– 36:1
Man is a fellow-worker with God.

108.   DEUTERONOMY 8:7–20
Spiritual dangers threaten a nation in times of material prosperity.

109.   DEUTERONOMY 26:1–11
Give thanks to God for all the good things he has given.

110.   1 CHRONICLES 29:1–13
All good things come from God, so natural resources and wealth are to be used to glorify God.

111.   2 CHRONICLES 5:1,13,14
Solomon builds God's temple. All work should be for the glory of God.

112.   NEHEMIAH 4
To build and create is hard; there are always critics and detractors.

113.   JOB 28:3–6, 9–15, 20, 23–28
The wise use of resources and technology.

114.   PROVERBS 3:1–6
Trust in God for all things, self-interest and self-importance have no place in God's kingdom.

115.   ISAIAH 44:6–23
The prophet reminds us how man, in his pride, makes perverted use of God's creation and his own talents.

116.   ISAIAH 45:1–13
God uses secular movements to do his work.

117.   ISAIAH 58:7–10
The prophet reminds us that work is not self-orientated; work is for those who are not able to help themselves.

118.   JEREMIAH 29:4–7
Jeremiah instructs the people in exile to play a full part

in the life of Babylon; in the same way Christians cannot opt out of the community of which they are part.

119.   EZEKIEL 37:1–14
The valley of dry bones comes to life through the Spirit of God. Likewise those dead parts of our life can be renewed through God's love.

120.   AMOS 5:6–15
The importance of justice and fairness in society. Those who work are to be fair in all their dealings.

121.   AMOS 5:14–24
True religion stresses justice for all, and so should be for the benefit of all.

122.   MICAH 4:1–7
Life is hallowed in the sight of God, and work in all forms is part of his purpose.

123.   MICAH 6:6–8
God has shown what is good. He requires justice and love, not the abundance of material things.

124.   HABAKKUK 2:1–4, 9–14
There should be justice for all. Those who work only for themselves and use others are condemned by God.

(ii) New Testament

125.   MATTHEW 6:1–6
All must be done with humility, remembering what God has already done for man.

126.   MATTHEW 6:19–24
Jesus shows the right attitude to earthly things. God's priorities are very different.

127.   MATTHEW 6:24–34
The right priorities of life, the proper importance of wealth and the desire of possessions.

128.   MATTHEW 7:1–12
All people are equal before God; petty jealousies are destructive for each has his or her part to play.

129.   MATTHEW 18:21–35
The importance of forgiveness. No one has a monopoly of goodness. In any dispute each party has wronged the other.

130.   MATTHEW 20:1–16
The parable of the labourers is a reminder of the destructiveness of greed.

131.   MATTHEW 25:14–29
The parable of the talents reminds us of the proper use of resources and skills.

132.   MATTHEW 25:31–45
The strong are to support the weak. Those who work come to help those who are needy.

133.   LUKE 4:14–21
Jesus cares and loves those whom we would rather not love. Business is to be about more than profit.

134.   LUKE 10:25–28
Love is the most important priority in living.

135.   LUKE 12:13–24
The poverty of wealth. If business is no more than making money, means are substituted for ends.

136.   JOHN 1:1–14
God's involvement with his creation is plain to see. The Gospel expresses his love and concern for the world.

137. JOHN 6:25–35
The importance of getting earthly things into perspective. Jesus tells of the right priority.

138. JOHN 13:3–17
Jesus's humility is an example for those who are in authority to be humble. All men are equal in the presence of God.

139. JOHN 14:15–27
The promise of the Holy Spirit is the promise of new life.

140. JOHN 21:1–14
The resurrection story reminds us how God may be seen in the everyday and commonplace.

141. ACTS 1:15–26
Important decisions require prayer.

142. ACTS 20:32–35
A good job requires a group to work together. Business should be governed by co-operation instead of self-interest.

143. ROMANS 8:1–8
St Paul reminds us of the right priorities of life, that material things are never an end in themselves.

144. ROMANS 8:14–17, 38–39
Through God's love man is freed from fear, liberated from the oppression of material things.

145. ROMANS 12:1–13
All people have their own gifts and so their own importance.

146. ROMANS 13:1–10
The right attitude to work, to be diligent and faithful.

147. 1 CORINTHIANS 3:3–9
We are all God's fellow-workers; competition leads
only to jealousy and strife; co-operation is God's way.

148. 1 CORINTHIANS 12:4–11
All forms of work are inspired by the Spirit of God and
so all are important.

149. 1 CORINTHIANS 12:12–27
All people have their part to play; co-operation in all
forms of work brings out the best in each.

150. 1 CORINTHIANS 15:49–58
The work of mankind is part of God's creation.

151. 2 CORINTHIANS 8:1–14
Abundance and equality. Those without wealth show
the wealthy riches in non-material things.

152. EPHESIANS 4:17–32
The whole of life is to be lived in the new way of Christ,
so all work is to be governed by God's love.

153. EPHESIANS 6:5–12
The right attitude to work and relationships. Attacks
should be against social evils rather than against any
individual.

154. PHILIPPIANS 2:1–11
The example of Jesus shows a better way to live and
work, which is glorified by God.

155. COLOSSIANS 1:11–20
All things come from God, are fulfilled in Jesus, and so
we should give thanks.

156. COLOSSIANS 3:1–17
The message of the Gospel is to stop being motivated
by self-interest and to put on God's love.

157. 1 THESSALONIANS 5:12–28
Peace and justice are essential to the Gospel. In this
new way each may work in the spirit of co-operation
instead of confrontation.

158. JAMES 4:13– 5:12
Self-interest is not acceptable. Affluence and wealth
carry a burden of responsibility.

159. 1 PETER 2:4–12
Through Jesus all have been raised to new life, and so
self-interest has no place in this new life.

160. 1 JOHN 4:7–21
'Love one another' is Jesus's command. This is the new
way of the Gospel and in this new way all may work in
peace and equality.

161. REVELATION 21:1–6
God in Jesus is with mankind in his work and suffering.

(iii) Apocrypha

162. WISDOM 6:1, 9, 11
Everyone is accountable for the exercise of authority
and power; those who govern, control and organise
should never act for themselves.

163. ECCLESIASTICUS 38:24–39
The high vocation of craftsmen. There is a need and
place for skilled work.

(b) Readings in subject order

(i) Co-operation not competition

See items numbered 124, 129, 142, 147, 149 and 157.

(ii)   Creation and new life

See items numbered 101, 119, 131, 136 and 139.

(iii)   Man spoils God's creation

See items numbered 103, 104, 115, 130 and 135.

(iv)   Right relationships

See items numbered 120, 125, 128, 152 and 160.

(v)   Right priorities

See items numbered 114, 126, 133, 143 and 156.

(vi)   Thanksgiving

See items numbered 109, 110, 111, 154 and 155.

(vii)   The responsibility of power

See items numbered 105, 138, 141, 158 and 162.

(viii)   The value of man

See items numbered 102, 107, 145, 149 and 161.

(ix)   The value of work

See items numbered 106, 122, 148, 150 and 163.

(x)   Work is for everyone's benefit

See items numbered 121, 124, 132, 151 and 153.

READINGS: NON-BIBLICAL

READINGS: NON-BIBLICAL

Christian management

164.   We also need a clearer idea of what the Bible has to say about management. It has a good deal more to say than I have ever heard said. I think our Lord was being a wonderful manager when he sent the 70 out and when he chose Judas Iscariot, whom he knew would betray him, because he told all of us who are managers that we must give initiative to others knowing that we will occasionally be let down, perhaps badly. There cannot be growth in any organisation or a sense of wholeness or justice unless people are given initiative. That is the manager's job, and initiative should flow both ways, and does in any good company. If we were to look at the New Testament from this point of view, I think we would see that we could deduce principles of efficient management from the way in which our Lord behaved towards his disciples, and the way in which the early Church set about its task of evangelism after our Lord's resurrection. So far as I know, nobody gave Stephen the right to preach, and nobody told Philip to go and run beside the eunuch. These men were given quite humble functions – to serve tables – by the Church, but they used those functions to witness to the eternal verities of the Christian faith, and became thereby the protomartyr and the proto-evangelist of the Christian Church. We can learn a lesson here, because we see here the infinite capacity of men to grow and to take challenges, and our job as managers, and especially as Christian managers, is to provide those challenges. The Church is not perhaps very good at this, and we laymen sometimes feel that there should be more giving and taking of initiative in the Church. In industry we understand it better. We now have what is called the 'Y' theory of participative management, and this means the giving and taking of challenges, and the validation of authority which comes from this, from the bottom as well as from the top.

Christianity and human relations in industry

165. Good human relations in industry can only be surely founded on the treatment of each individual as a human personality whose welfare in the highest sense must be regarded as an end in itself. It is specially necessary to emphasise this point today when, in view of the desperate need to increase production, a new and intensified interest is being focused on all those conditions which affect industrial morale and people's will to work. This increased interest is all to the good, and one can see a bright side to the present emergency in that it has brought about such an awakening. But the interest once aroused must be of the right kind. If managers start now to take a human interest in the workers merely in order to improve production results, then they will be both wrong and unsuccessful. They will be wrong because regard for human beings should be seen as an end in itself. They will be unsuccessful because they will be found out. The whole industrial field is bedevilled with suspicions based on past memories. As a result, even the most honest attempts to improve human relations tend to be viewed with mistrust – either as dodges to get something extra out of the workers for the benefit of the profit-makers or as signs of a temporary mood 'produced by force of circumstances rather than a change of heart' (to quote words recently used to me by a trade union leader). If the success of genuine attempts is threatened by suspicion, bogus attempts will certainly fail.

Common purpose

166. 'Men do not live by bread alone' (Deut. 8:3). We certainly need bread, but we also need something more. If we are to work together in industry and not let our very natural differences divide us, we must see in our work a greater sense of common purpose.

What is this sense which can be blessed by God and which can win the minds and hearts of people? Is not our common purpose at work the creation of 'worth'? At work we create not just the goods and services that people need, but also jobs and incomes which give people self-respect and set us free. We create revenue through taxation which pays nurses, social services and pensions. We create investment so that future generations may continue to benefit. We create exports to help countries overseas – that revenue in turn enables us to buy their products and give them employment. And lastly, we create a return on people's savings.

As Christians we spend too much time decrying the mistakes of industry – whether because of strife or strikers or because of its effects on the environment – perhaps we should recognise that not only does work need man, but also that man needs work.

May we in our lives see how we can bring back some sense of mission to work. And may God bless our strivings in industry and commerce to create worth – for the very basis of worship is offering true worth to God.

Creative work

167. It is easy but wrong to glamorise the Bible's view of work. Man, 'in the image of God', is made to fulfil himself in creative activity. This belongs to his high destiny. But there is no sentimentality here. Human toil has been 'cursed' through the Fall. The consequences are reflected in working conditions; it will be by 'the sweat of his brow'.

Many of us here are privileged. We experience our work as a high dignity, as something in which we can rejoice. Many others do not. Their work is dull. It is exhausting – not healthily so but just debilitating. There are many whose problem is that of no work and their numbers will swell through the impact of new developments.

The work of man, now as when Moses was called, belongs in the realm of God's redemption. The Church must take seriously its place within that plan; ministry and laity sharing together in uplifting all who labour, seeking to renew the institution of industrial life and holding before all the promise of a brighter future.

One contemporary word is of special import; the word, 'Technology'. It conjures many fears for some people. Understandably! It will cause hardship for the moment. But is that all? Maybe the scientists and technologists of our age have been raised up by God for the redemption of his people, even if, like Cyrus, they know him not!

Used according to the Divine Will, the new instruments they have produced may liberate from drudgery, end dehumanisation and lead to a new Promised Land. It may not flow with milk and honey but it can be a true community in which we are freed from meaningless toil for the real, creative work of caring for each other.

Economic freedom

168. The existing system has many triumphs to its credit; it has raised the standard of life of the common people to a level never reached before. The life of the 'working people' is for the most part neither impoverished, nor over-burdensome, nor lacking in interest. But it suffers from one great lack, from one common evil, and from one terrible menace. The great lack is the absence of any voice in the control or direction of the concern to which most of the waking hours of the day are given. Till this can be remedied there will be one most important respect in which the working class is shut out from a vitally important expression of personality. Men have fought and died for a voice in making the laws they have to obey: that is the essence of political liberty.

But the government of the firm for which he works affects a man's life more closely than the Government of his State. Yet in it he has no part except so far as he may threaten to hold up the process by withdrawing his labour and that of his fellow-workers in a strike. In many businesses today the workers are often consulted, especially about regulations affecting hours and conditions of work. So far, so good: but this is done as a favour and not as a matter of secured right. The cause of freedom will not be established till political freedom is fulfilled in economic freedom.

Moreover, until this is done, the breach of fellowship – of which the class war is the ultimate expression – must remain.

Encountering light

169. But Christians cannot play for safety, and those who are held by God can afford to be daring. Some are called to go out and meet danger in obvious ways, encountering the hatred and sickness and depression of people in desperate need. Others are called to face and deal with some much less obvious danger. If you are very rich it could be much more dangerous to live with the money and try to use it properly and responsibly than to give it all away. Or if you are an assembly-line worker in a factory it could be much riskier going on there, trying to be Christ in that place and to bring his healing to a system that turns men into machines, than escaping into an easy, less destructive job.

Of course, if you are following Christ you will find

danger in whatever your vocation turns out to be, just as you will also find the drudgery and pain, and the joy and fulfilment of carrying a cross. It is possible to serve him wherever you are and whatever your work happens to be. Social workers and clergy and teachers are not doing a more 'Christian' job than bus conductors or civil servants or bricklayers – in fact they may have a softer option. It can be most terrifyingly difficult to learn to find meaning in life and to see God and serve him when you are living and working in the greed and pressure and ugliness of industrial and commercial life.

God wants us

170.   God wants us to do good work at whatever job we are working. He expects us to work as diligently and skilfully as we possibly can.

God wants us to exhibit love in our relationships with our fellow workers and our employers.

God wants us to seek ways to be of service to others in our working place and through our work. When he sees something which needs to be done, a Christian should be quick to volunteer himself to do it. He should not seek to escape from serving.

God wants us to work actively for justice and righteousness in our working place. If there is suffering or wrong or any bad conditions, the Christian must work energetically to find ways to bring justice and righteousness to his working place and to improve the welfare of his fellow workers.

God wants us to tell those who work with us about his gospel; if they do not yet know him, he wants us to bring them to faith in him.

God's world

171.   God's engineering is much more subtle, so much more complex and sophisticated than mine. Its output is perpetual. The plant never breaks down. It works steadily by day – powerfully and noiselessly – and it rests by night. Its variety is legion; yet each element works in perfect harmony with all others, and all its waste-products are recycled. At all times the total production system is in equilibrium, and yet each part is in a perpetual state of development. So long as the sun shines it needs nothing to drive it; and it never wears out because it constantly renews itself. From raw material to finished product – atoms to molecules; molecules to cells or crystals; cells to fibres or muscle, crystals to rocks – the production system is fully automated. Yet each individual product is unique – 'Heaven and earth are full of thy glory!'

He took bread

172. It is the false separation of the material from the spiritual which leads many Christians today to think that they can only be true or real Christians if they give up their work in the world, especially if that work is in industry or in commerce, and seek ordination or pursue the religious life of a monk or a nun or at least take up some non-materialistic career in teaching, nursing or other form of social work. They make us all feel that those who work at making things, or digging things out of the ground or out of the sea, or by distributing those things through transport and trade – in short, those who work in industry and commerce – are in some sort of way only second-class Christians.

The supreme Christian teaching on the unity of the spiritual and the material is surely in the Christian understanding of what we call the incarnation. In Jesus Christ we see God in man made manifest – made obvious – made evident to the eye, the mind and to our judgement. The spiritual embodied in the material. So in this central Christian teaching we are shown that the spiritual and the material cannot be separated.

Then as if to reinforce that teaching, in that great moment when our Lord himself institutes the central and most profound act of Christian worship – the Eucharist, the Mass, Holy Communion, the Lord's Supper, whatever we may call it, at what we best know as the Last Supper – he picks up a piece of bread and he takes into his hand a cup of wine. He takes up these most material things, these products of man's agriculture and manufacture – not natural products but products which are the fruits of man's inventiveness – human artifacts – and with these things he gives thanks and offers them as his Body and his Blood. The spiritual incorporated in the material.

I believe that if we can hold firm to that great Christian understanding of the co-equal nature of the spiritual and the material, if we can see that we, very material creatures, are spiritual creatures as well, then we can grasp another great truth which flows from that understanding. It is that to play a part in producing the material needs of people through our work is one of the most perfect ways in which we can serve God. Those who engage in the production and distribution of the material things of life through agriculture, through manufacture or through mining in all its modern forms, together with those who distribute those products through transport and commerce, perform a profoundly Christian service.

Human labour

173.   There is universal agreement that a fundamental source of human wealth is human labour. Now a modern economist has been brought up to consider 'labour' or work as little more than a necessary evil. From the point of view of the employer an item of cost to be reduced to a minimum if not eliminated. From the point of view of the workman to work is to sacrifice one's leisure and comfort. The ideal with regard to

work is to get rid of it. The Buddhist view of work is threefold: to give man a chance to utilise and develop his faculties, to enable him to overcome his egocentredness by joining with other people in a common task, to bring forth the goods and services needed for a becoming existence. To organise work in such a manner that it becomes meaningless, boring, stultifying or nerve-wracking for the worker would be little short of criminal; it would indicate a greater concern with goods than with people, an evil lack of compassion and a soul-destroying degree of attachment to the most primitive side of this worldly existence.

Human work

174. Just as human activity proceeds from man, so it is ordered towards man; for when a man works, he not only alters things and society, he develops himself as well. He learns much, he cultivates his resources, he goes outside of himself and beyond himself. Rightly understood, this kind of growth is of greater value than any external riches which can be garnered. Hence the norm of human activity is this: that in accord with the divine plan and will, it should harmonise with the genuine good of the human race, and allow people as individuals and as members of society, to pursue their total vocation and fulfil it.

A person is more precious for what he is than for what he has. Similarly, all that people do to obtain greater justice, wider brotherhood, and a more humane ordering of social relationships has greater worth than technical advances; for these advances can supply the material for human progress, but of themselves they can never actually bring it about.

Inspiring the main army: a Christian challenge

175. The work of the Church is seen 'in the sphere of providing succour for the non-combatants and the wounded, not inspiring the main army', says R. H. Tawney, as a criticism of the Church, in his book 'Religion and the Rise of Capitalism'. Are there things which the Churches can say or do which might 'inspire the main army' of those involved in industry or commerce? What follows are not ten new commandments but ten pieces of Christian ammunition for the army.

1. *Work is service*, not self-interest. The example of Jesus is that of a servant who tried to meet the differing needs of all who come to him. The purpose of a company should be to serve customers, employees, share-holders and the wider community.

2. *Work is stewardship*, not exploitation. God made mankind to be stewards of his creation. This implies the responsibility to use the earth's resources wisely and to apply investment, research and development to areas of greatest need.

3. *Work is fulfilling*, not frustrating. We are made in the image of a creator God. Therefore we need to feel an element of creativity and sense of achievement in some parts of our work. The introduction of new technologies and new work practices needs to take this into account.

4. *Work is competitive*. We have to believe in what we are doing. Jesus and his first disciples had to earn a place for their beliefs against strong opposition. British industry will need to believe that its objectives are the right ones before it can

compete in international markets and wipe out
unemployment at home. Christians must be involved in creating new objectives for industry if
they want to have a voice in how benefits will be
redistributed.

5. *Work is compassionate.* Jesus had a particular
concern for the poor and the weak. Any humane
society must make provision for those who cannot compete on equal terms. The redundant and
the unemployed have to be allowed to find new
ways of gaining self-respect.

6. *Work has to be earned.* Jesus paid a very high
price for his beliefs. In Britain we are going
through a painful economic transition. There
cannot be the right to work unless there is the
economic and political will to create new jobs. To
use the language of the resurrection hope: our
industries could just die, or they could rise again
with a transformed life.

7. *Work is not private.* Jesus' second commandment
is that we should love our neighbours as
ourselves. In a world of great specialisation we
have become increasingly interdependent. Good
teamwork has to be a facet of life. Powerful
groups have come to exert great influence. With
great power exercised by management, unions,
transnational companies, banks and governments goes great responsibility. In a very real
sense, I am my brother's keeper.

8. *Work corrupts.* No one is perfect: there seems to
be a fault in the way that we are made. Christians
call it sin. Individuals and companies fail to live
up to their own ideals. It is important to be open
to scrutiny and accountable to others. Humility
goes with maturity.

9. *Work is not everything.* Christians believe that wholeness comes through a balanced life. A person with a range of interests contributes more to work and to society. Family life, personal development, hobbies, are all part of what we need to be complete people. Broad interests may make unemployment or retirement easier to accept.

10. *Work is judgement.* We are judged by others and will be judged by God on the standards by which we live. What we, or a company, actually do, says much about what is really believed. We cannot earn our own salvation but we do have to live responsibly.

Meditation on a sliced loaf

176. Today we get our bread from the supermarket. From a stack of plastic-wrapped packs we take one, identical with its fellows. What is in it, we can neither see nor feel – we only know from the fatuous legend on the bag. We place it in a wire trolley, along with other, equally unrecognisable, packs and tins, and join a queue of strangers at the check-out. Our money is accepted, the change given, a slip of paper from the till handed over, to protect us from the unwelcome attentions of the store detective; and the whole transaction is completed with perhaps no more than a perfunctory 'Ta, Love'. Where the bread comes from, who baked it, what flour (milled by whom? from whose grain?) went into it, nobody either knows or cares. What other ingredients it contains, far better not ask: and anyway, you know what flour is – but what on earth is monosodium glutamate? When we come to eat the bread, we no longer even have to cut it – yet what an adventure of tactile discovery that used to be! Instead, a flabby, homogeneous piece of glutinous tile flops out of the plastic bag.

This loaf serves only one purpose: to fill some space in the human interior. That apart, it neither tastes good nor nourishes the body. All that network of experiences and relationships that used to surround a loaf of bread has gone. This loaf barely has a place in creation, for little binds it to anything else and gives it a context. Worse, our place in creation is also by that much less assured, less definable. For we are bound to a crusty loaf, by taste, by smell, by touch, by sight, by sound – and by love for those who made it. That is all lost – and a few of the bonds which gave us a context and a place in God's world are severed. By a strange inversion, a self-indulgent pursuit of the cheap and the labour-saving has produced a withdrawal from the world – a kind of sterile asceticism.

People versus machines

177. The coming of computers – like the coming of the prophets of old overthrowing the idols – tells us that if we have put our trust in princes, if we have put our trust in the princes of the mind, by being able to do things cleverly, if we put our trust in the princes of the body, by being able to do things with great strength and physical skill, we are putting our trust in idols. So that in a society which really values that which is human and which judges people by their attainments as human creatures, there is no possible reason to fear the machine. The machine by definition is the servant of humanity. Where fear of the machine comes, it is a sign that there is already inhumanity in the social structure, and therefore to this degree the fear of the machine is the most intense barometer society can have of injustice of that which, as Christians we should say, was under the judgement of God. The basic point I want to make is that insofar as we build the social structure in which people are valued as people, that social structure is one in which there can be no fear of machines, no fear of the computers taking over. What we are valuing in people is something which the machine cannot do.

Religion and life

178. In any slum parish in any large town, or in an industrial parish such as Jarrow or Tonypandy before the war, the Evangelist proclaims that God is Love, while all the evidence around him denies the truth of his assertion. In any industrial parish the preacher declares that man is made in the image of God, that he is an immortal soul with an eternal destiny, whereas the man himself is involved in a system which regards him as a mechanical robot – a human machine whose primary function is to produce and consume the product of industrial activity. We talk to men about the dignity of work and the vocation of industry – that they are fellow-workers with God – when they have no freedom of choice in the work they do, no room for craftsmanship or personal expression in the deadly monotony of the conveyor belt, and no security beyond the personal whim of the employer or the uncertain demands of a fluctuating market. The result is, as Dr Temple said, that man has come to be regarded, and even regards himself, as only that part of the machine which no one has yet invented.

Statement about industrial mission

179. Most people spend a large part of their lives at work. It is both their livelihood and a means by which they find, or fail to find, dignity and fulfilment. The Christian Church believes that men and women share in God's creative work and are responsible for a wise ordering of this world. It is important that they should develop these powers in the work they do and that industry should provide the community with goods and services which it needs. Industry should be for people and not people for industry.

Industry is one of the most important and influential institutions in our society. Deep conflicts arise as a result of developments in technology, world trade and people's expectations – conflicts between wealth and poverty, quantity and quality, work and frustration, concentrations of power and participation. If these conflicts are to be resolved, wisdom and vision and the courage to change and be changed will be required from every section of society. It is because the Christian Church believes that there are resources making these conflicts creative, and wishes to share in enabling men and women to experience their full responsibilities, that it engages in industrial mission.

Industrial Mission is one aspect of the Church's work in which all denominations co-operate. The industrial chaplain seeks to develop relationships of mutual confidence with personnel and welfare officers, heads of departments and trade union representatives. The team of chaplains convenes groups and conferences for management, trade unions, the Church and other organisations for discussion of industrial, social and religious issues. They commit themselves, as Christians, to social policies which they believe will lead to greater security, a fairer distribution of wealth and income, a wider sharing of responsibility, and a better quality of life.

The alienation of the Church from the industrial worker

180. It is patently true that the Church has the slenderest roots in the life of the industrial community. There is hardly any active opposition to the Church; on the contrary, there is an immense amount of goodwill both for the Church and her clergy. This is much better than the situation in other European countries, where there

is often active hostility, although the gap between the Church and industrial society is enormous even in our own country. We must realise how far contemporary industrial man, especially at the lower levels of industry, is removed from being actively identified with the worship and way of life of the Church.

In so far as the working man thinks about the Church at all, he sees it on the other side of the fence from where he stands. It represents another class, not necessarily one he hates; his circle is outside it; it is the done thing for his group not to go to church, and he is seldom prepared to break with the commonly accepted practices of his mates. He identifies the Church with the suburbs, with a different way of life and a different kind of speech. He knows that the lay people who serve in the councils of the Church are not drawn from his class. If he remembers anything about religion at all, he thinks of it as a pious moralism, at the most all right for the wife and kids, but not really of much significance for the world in which his life is set. I believe that this fact, which if anything I have understated, constitutes the greatest challenge to our Church.

The calling to lay ministry

181. To be called to lay service is to be called to live fully in the secular world, to be at ease in it, to know its idiom and its assumptions, to engage in its arguments and affairs, because one's centre is there. It is not to sally out from one's 'real' centre, the parish church and its affairs, or the diocesan structures, for sorties into industry or trade or education or politics or whatever. It is to live in industry or trade or education or politics, to earn one's income from them (or be unemployed by them); to be committed to them; and there, in that place where one's energies are committed, to engage quite consciously in mission and ministry. It is to see oneself as committed for work outside the 'club' of the

Church in its parishes and diocesan structures, with no responsibility whatever for maintaining them. Rather, it is the responsibility of the parishes and diocesan structures to maintain spiritually such lay missionaries, as a sort of secret army for God working out on the boundaries. All such lay ministers ought to be commissioned by their parishes and sent out to their task, and then supported by weekly prayer for them in the parish church, by counselling, and by a support group within the parish/deanery. But their function is not to keep the Church going as an institution, but to draw their support, comfort, sustenance and theological depth from it as they work in Christ's name in their secular calling.

The Christian in industrial society

182. The Christian's task is to participate in the modern life without worshipping it. The Christian view of life, I believe, is the only rational one, and if this is so the Christian will understand matters better than the worshipper of the rate of growth and should be able to exercise a far-reaching influence on account of his more perfect understanding.

For example, the Christian knows that it is not rational to choose a 'rate of economic growth' as one's objective. 'Growth' is a purely quantitative concept and therefore has no real meaning at all. It may be a great Good or a great Evil. What is to grow, by what means, and to whose benefit? 'Labour-saving', too, is a purely quantitative concept and therefore a meaningless aim; so is 'automation' or 'cybernation'. These things may be very good or very evil. What kind of labour is to be saved? Whose labour? Most terms of economics are purely quantitative and therefore unreal and meaningless.

It is not rational to treat work simply as a 'disutility' and a means to an end. This is the great untruth of the religion of economics. If people do not know this as Christians, they should know it from observation. Uncreative, repetitive work, if done without intelligible purpose, is indeed an evil and should be eliminated by 'labour-saving'; but it is madness to eliminate creative work either by automation or by turning it into uncreative work for the sake of productivity. The private, profit-seeking point of view may here be completely incompatible with the general mood. Without creative work, man cannot be man.

The Christian view of human life

183. Man is created for fellowship in the family of God: fellowship first with God, and through that with all of God's children. And that is the primary test that must be applied to every system that is constructed and every change in the system that is proposed. Does it help us nearer towards fullness and richness of personal fellowship? And fellowship, of course, is not merely the same thing as all getting together and agreeing with one another: it is compatible with a great deal of disagreement, and with a great deal of variety of experience.

Well, now, the real goods of life are all in personal qualities and personal relationships: the fullness of personal existence, the width of interest, spiritual, intellectual, imaginative, and the rest, and the relationships with our neighbours, and our friends – these are the things that really constitute the substance of human life, to which everything else ought all the while to be subordinated. And it is very hard, when the apparatus of life, so to speak, begins to be extremely complicated, to maintain that subordination; our business mechanism and our financial mechanism are become so elaborate that those who work them are bound to give an immense amount of time and attention to the mere process of keeping them in order. And that makes it very hard to avoid falling into the error of making these things ends in themselves. They claim so much attention during life that it is very difficult to remember that, after all, their whole value lies in the service they can render to something beyond themselves.

The Church and the world economic crisis

184. So I believe our economic ills today are the outcome of a profound moral disturbance of the world. It is not our lack of economic sense, or our inability to invent and create that has landed us in the difficulties which have almost overwhelmed us. It is rather our lack of control, our inability to harness to good and wise purposes the tremendous forces that mankind has created by ingenuity and research. High explosives, aircraft, atomic power, these are the fine flowers of human endeavour, they are the trophies won in the unending struggle to master the forces of nature, and we should be proud of them, we should delight in them; instead we fear them for the evil purposes to which they have been and may be put. Economic domination and competitive acquisitiveness are today so often the controlling influence in the use of these great forces that we have developed; they represent the misapplied ambitions of mankind based on materialist selfishness.

The Church's affirmation of work

185. We know, when we stop to think, that we are dependent on industry, and yet we are unable to affirm industrial life as being of real worth. This is a basic sickness at the heart of our society, a failure in our fundamental attitudes. Put in religious terms, we are unable to relate our belief in the creative power and purpose of God to the existence of factories and mills and power stations and office blocks. In an agricultural society, praise is given to God for his power in the rhythm of seed-time and harvest, for his mercy in the fresh growth each year of grain and crops. Even today harvest festival exercises an attraction even in the most urban of parishes surrounded by brick for miles and without a field or farm within its boundaries. Where is the corresponding affirmation of God at work within the industrial process? A piece of coal amidst the apples in the sanctuary, or a cog wheel among the chrysanthemums is nothing more than a reluctant admission that our lives today depend upon coal and cogs, upon oil and computers as much as upon crops and cattle. We need a joyful celebration of the worth of the industrial undertaking, a celebration which must have its religious aspect. When a Festival of Industry touches our hearts as deeply as does harvest festival, then we shall have overcome our sickness. Just as individuals cannot live in a healthy way if they deny part of themselves, if they believe that a significant part of themselves is evil, so societies cannot live in a healthy way if they believe that a significant part of their social life is somehow evil; or even if they feel that it is dubious. There is nothing dubious about converting the wealth of resources with which God has endowed this world into means by which man may live and realise the purposes for which God has created him.

The meaning of worship

186.   'Worship God? Why should I? I'm as good as many who do go to church and perhaps not such a hypocrite. I can worship God when I go out for a walk in the country, if I want to. And after all – does God really want people to go to church and sing hymns and psalms to him? Isn't he far too big and great and far away to want anything of the kind? I don't believe he wants to be flattered by people who think they are good and are no better than most of us.'

Crowds of people think in this way about worship. And yet, in spite of the bit of truth in it all, worship is a far greater and more glorious thing than anyone who thinks like this can ever have understood.

Worship is much wider than anything which we offer to God in the services of the Church appears to be at first sight. It has to do with the whole of creation. In the worship which we give to God in church we enter into this wider worship and see how the whole of life can become worship.

The material world is also made to give its response to God, but in many cases it can only do so when man uses material things rightly. God has given all that man needs for his life in his gifts to men in the earth. Men have taken these and used them selfishly and wrongly, as if they did not belong to God. They have used iron for making guns and chemicals for poison gas, and bread for making profit, and they have forgotten that these are God's gifts for the upbuilding of all men's lives. If man will worship God fully, and consciously fulfil his purposes, he must learn to direct the use of things to their right end as part of his life of worship.

The primary social services

187.   We value and give thanks for education and for medicine.

But what would education be without pen and ink, books and printing presses. What would pens be without the factories that make them and the plant that produced the materials from which they are made. What would printing presses be without the power stations that drive them, the oil refineries that lubricate them and the steel works that turn rock into the metal from which they are shaped.

And what would medicine be without the surgeons' instruments and the sterilising equipment that makes them safe to use. What terrors would an operation hold were it not for the factories that produce the anaesthetists' equipment and the chemicals that allow it to proceed painlessly.

How can we give thanks for education and medicine without also giving thanks for all the many material things without which they could not exist.

Are not industry and commerce the primary social services on which all else depends?

The sharing of power

188. Concentration of power in a few hands means that decisions are taken without reference to the views of those most affected and there is bound to be injustice where a man is a means to someone else's end. He is being treated as an object rather than a subject. It is often said that those who are frustrated within industry have ample opportunities to recover their influence and prestige in social life outside working hours. It is true that work is made for man and not man for work, and that in the future much more attention must be given to the promotion of leisure interests. But this is really no answer to our problem. If men are to be made whole and their potential realised, we must recognise that the act of judgement is central for a maturing personality. It is a part of his freedom as a human being. He cannot be expected to act responsibly or to carry out instructions willingly unless he is treated as an adult person. Some of the practical difficulties in the way are mentioned above but to abandon respect for personality is only to create insuperable difficulties in the long run.

However, Christians more than others will realise that human limitations make the achievement of industrial and indeed any sort of democracy which is worth while a long and difficult process. Christian faith recognises that however good a programme is envisaged men can sink to depths of selfishness. Inordinate desire, excessive individualism and blind pursuit of sectional interests are often at the root of industrial strife. Jesus emphasised the place of dominant desire in the human heart. Where monetary incentives take over complete control, concern for social justice can recede into the background. What begins as a crusade ends as a struggle from which no one benefits. Directors, investors, managers, workers are capable of the worst as well as the best. This does not imply cynicism about human progress, because human nature can be cleansed, restored and renewed.

The 'worth' of the worker

189. As Christians we are concerned with Christ's message of loving, helping, caring and giving. As a society we are ahead of many others in our standard of material living and providing caring and compassionate services for people.

Perhaps we too often forget that we cannot have these goods and services, houses and hospitals, schools and old age pensions, unless people have first made them or created the wealth to pay for them.

Those who work in industry and commerce are in the business of creating those things that people need – creating not just the wealth, but the 'worth' for our society as well. The world of the Gospels is peopled by workers in vineyards, tax gatherers, fishermen and publicans – Christ himself was a carpenter. Perhaps we have seen the 'worth' of joining the local authority to help allocate houses to those in need, without also recognising the 'worth' of joining the construction company to help build them first.

We need industry and the talents of those who work in it to create what is needed for our caring society. The challenge is that at present we are not even paying for what we as a society are consuming.

And yet, the frustration of so many people is not that they are over-worked, over-stretched or over-used, but that they are under-needed, under-rated and under-used.

St Thomas Aquinas, 700 years ago, wrote: 'It is highly immoral to misuse people, highly immoral to under-use people or abuse them – but highly moral to call forth and make use of gifts that are in people.'

When possessions become curses

190. Christ never said it was impossible for a rich man to enter into the Kingdom of God; he said it was difficult, but that all things were possible with God. And that's just it. For a rich man or a rich people there are many more ways of going to the dogs or the devil than there are for poor men and for poor people, and therefore their need for God is more desperate.

For special people and for special reasons it may be a good thing to sell all that you have, give to the poor, and set forth in the strength of your naked personality to follow the ascetic way.

There have always been heroes who did this and the world owes them much; but it is not, and it is not meant to be, the ordinary way of life. It is not even of necessity the highest way of life, though it may very well be the way that individual men and women are called upon to take.

It is certainly not in every case the hardest way of life. Christ saw that clearly, and warned men that to accept gifts at God's hands made it absolutely necessary, if they were not to prove a curse rather than a blessing, that they should be received on bended knee and with heartfelt gratitude.

Work is toil

191. The fallen condition of man described in Genesis 3:17–20 is an all too familiar picture for any reluctant gardener! There is no gainsaying that most work is toil and drudgery. However, in the light of the life and death of the incarnate Son of God this condition acquires a new perspective. Our God is not Almighty in the sense that he works without struggle or effort or pain in order to achieve his will. Indeed through his incarnation he suffered the ultimate of torment and pain in his saving work, only to emerge triumphant and Almighty in the end.

Geoffrey Studdert Kennedy put it clearly and forcefully when he said: 'When we say that God is Almighty we don't mean that he has no obstacles to overcome, no problems to solve, and no pain to bear; but we declare our faith that he is strong enough and patient enough to overcome all obstacles, endure all pain and solve all problems and so prove himself Almighty in the end.'

If we are to share, through work, in his creative processes we surely cannot expect to be inoculated against striving and struggling and toiling; taking knocks as well as getting a kick from our endeavours. That is a real partnership in creation. Broad is the gate and easy the road that leads to destruction. The Cross is part of God's creative and redemptive processes.

SENTENCES

(a) Biblical
(b) Non-biblical

SENTENCES

(a) Biblical

192. Then God said, 'Let us make man in our image, after our likeness, and let them have dominion over the fish of the sea, and over the birds of the air, and over the cattle and over all the earth, and over every creeping thing that creeps upon the earth.' (Gen. 1:26)

193. Where were you when I laid the foundation of the earth? Who determined its measurements? Or who stretched the line upon it? On what were its bases sunk, or who laid its cornerstone, when the morning stars sang together, and all the sons of God shouted for joy? (Job 38:4–7)

194. God will give us his good gifts, and our land will yield its fruit. (Ps. 85:12)

195. May the goodness of the Lord be upon us, may he prosper the work of our hands. (Ps. 90:17)

196. The earth is filled with the gifts of the Lord: wine and oil and bread, to strengthen us and cheer our hearts. (Ps. 104:13,15)

197. Do not contend with a man for no reason, when he has done you no harm. Do not envy a man of violence and do not choose any of his ways; for the perverse man is an abomination to the Lord, but the upright are in his confidence. (Prov. 3:30–32)

198. Seek good and not evil, that you may live, and so the Lord, the God of hosts, will be with you. (Amos 5:14)

199. What does the Lord require of you but to do justice, and to love kindness, and to walk humbly with your God. (Mic. 6:8)

200. You are the light of the world. Let your light so shine before men, that they may see your good works and give glory to your Father who is in heaven. (Matt. 5:14,16)

201. For what does it profit a man, to gain the whole world and forfeit his life? (Mark 8:36)

202. Whoever would be great among you must be your servant, and whoever would be first among you must be slave of all. (Mark 10:44)

203. Judge not, and you will not be judged; condemn not and you will not be condemned; forgive and you will be forgiven. (Luke 6:37)

204. Where your treasure is, there will be your heart also. (Luke 12:34)

205. Everyone who exalts himself will be humbled, and he who humbles himself will be exalted. (Luke 14:11)

206. Do not labour for the food which perishes, but for the food which endures to eternal life. (John 6:27)

207. Do not be conformed to this world but be transformed by the renewal of your mind, that you may prove what is the will of God, what is good, acceptable and perfect. (Rom. 12:2)

208. We who are strong enough ought to bear with the failing of the weak, and not to please ourselves; let each of us please his neighbour for his good, to edify him. (Rom. 15:1)

209. We are God's fellow-workers; you are God's field, God's building. (1 Cor. 3:9)

210. Be steadfast, immovable, always abounding in the work of the Lord, knowing that in the Lord your labour is not in vain. (1 Cor. 15:58)

211. As a matter of equality your abundance at the present time should supply their want, so that their abundance may supply your want, that there may be equality. (2 Cor. 8:14)

212. He who sows sparingly will also reap sparingly, and he who sows bountifully will also reap bountifully. (2 Cor. 9:6)

213. Do not be deceived; God is not mocked, for whatever a man sows, that will he also reap. For he who sows to his own flesh will from the flesh reap corruption; but he who sows to the Spirit will from the Spirit reap eternal life. (Gal. 6:7)

214. Let all bitterness and wrath and anger and clamour and slander be put away from you, with all malice, and be kind to one another, tenderhearted, forgiving one another, as God in Christ forgave you. (Eph. 4:31–32)

215. Rejoice in the Lord always; again I will say, Rejoice. (Phil. 4:4)

216. Let the peace of Christ rule in your hearts, to which indeed you were called into one body, and be thankful. (Col. 3:15)

(b) Non-biblical

217. God has to be discovered in the situation, it is in and through the people we meet, the day-to-day happenings of life . . . that God comes to us.

218. If we idolise wealth we create poverty; if we idolise success then we create the inadequate; if we idolise power we create powerlessness.

219. If you want to go places, start from where you are;
If you are poor, start with something cheap;
If you are uneducated, start with something simple;
If you live in a poor environment, where the market is small, start with something small;
If you are unemployed, start using your labour power; any productive use of it is better than letting it lie idle.

220. In Britain you have a worse kind of poverty. A poverty of loneliness, of being unwanted, a poverty of the spirit. And that is the worst disease in the world today.

221. It is highly immoral to misuse people, highly immoral to underuse people or abuse them – but highly moral to call forth and make use of gifts that are in people.

222. Love meant something when things got mended.

223. Man is created for fellowship in the family of God: fellowship first with God, and through that with all of God's children.

224. No one says 'Good Morning' to the dustman.

225. No one will heed the messages of an absent Church.

226. No race can prosper till it learns there is as much dignity in tilling a field as in writing a poem.

227. Our love for our brother is the test of our love for God.

228. Our privileges can be no greater than our obligations. The protection of our rights can endure no longer than the performance of our responsibilities.

229. Since it is through man's labour that not only 'the fruits of our activity' but also that 'human dignity, brotherhood and freedom' must increase on earth, let the Christian know the place his work has not only in earthly progress but also in the development of the Kingdom of God.

230. Take time to think, it is the source of power.
Take time to play, it is the source of youth.
Take time to pray, it is the greatest power on earth.

231. The pursuit of wealth as an end in itself creates an atmosphere in which right social relations are hardly attainable and in which it is difficult not merely for the rich but for all classes to enter the Kingdom of Heaven.

232. The teaching of Christianity is binding upon men not only in their personal and domestic conduct, but in their economic and industrial organisation. It is the duty of the Christian Church to urge that considerations of Christian morality must be applied to all such social relationships.

233. The value of a man
is not what he is in and for himself (Humanism)
nor what he is for society (Fascism and Communism)
but what he is worth to God.
  That is the principle of Christian equality:
  the supreme importance of every man is that
  he is the brother for whom Christ died.

234. Whether our work is art or science or the daily work of society, it is only the form in which we explore our experience which is different.

235. Without creative work, man cannot be man.

236. Work is a good thing for man – a good thing for his humanity – because through work he not only transforms nature, adapting it to his own needs, but he also achieves fulfilment as a human being and indeed, in a sense, becomes 'more than a human being'.

HYMNS AND SONGS

(a) Hymns found in a selection of hymnbooks
(b) Hymns not found in the selection of hymnbooks
(c) Psalms
(d) Hymns and songs suggested for various subjects

HYMNS AND SONGS

(a) Hymns found in a selection of hymnbooks

The Key to the abbreviations used in the table below is on page 126. The numbers in the table refer to the hymn numbers in the hymnbooks concerned.

	AHH FT	AMR	BHB	CP	EH	HS	HF TC	MHB	SP
237. A brighter dawn is breaking					126				435
238. All creatures of our God and King		172	1	31				28	439
239. All my hope on God is founded			492	417			451	70	442
240. All people that on earth do dwell	3	166	2	1	365		14	2	443
241. All who love and serve your city						3			
242. Angel voices, ever singing		246	4	279			307	668	
243. At the name of Jesus	225		199	167	368		172		392
244. Before Thy throne, O God, we kneel								884	
245. Behold us, Lord, a little space		13	627	277				949	39
246. Believe not those who say				521				591	453
247. Be Thou my Vision, O Lord of my heart	10		462	432				632	
248. Blessed city, heavenly Salem				169			559	190	
249. Blest are the pure in heart		335	463	446	370		110	950	455

	AHH FT	AMR	BHB	CP	EH	HS	HF TC	MHB	SP
250. Christ is our corner-stone		243	627				564	702	464
251. Come down, O Love Divine		235	224	204	152		231	273	177
252. Come, Holy Ghost, our hearts inspire		157	244	226			589	305	178
253. Come to us creative spirit							308		
254. Come, workers for the Lord	17					2			
255. Come, ye thankful people, come		482	724	645	289			962	9
256. Creator of the earth and skies	18					15	320		44
257. Crown him upon the throne									480
258. Dear Lord and Father of mankind		184	50	408	383		356	669	431
259. Father, hear the prayer we offer									
260. Father, Lord of all creation	23	182	467	523	385		360		487
261. Father of all! whose powerful voice								47	
262. Fill thou my life, O Lord my God		373	628	22			541	604	492
263. For the beauty of the earth		171	8	37	309		298	35	494
264. For the fruits of His creation							286		
265. For the healing of the nations	28								
266. Forth in thy name, O Lord, I go		336	629	593	259		306	590	29
267. From you all skill and science flow			635				310		
268. God is love, his the care							311		502

	AHH FT	AMR	BHB	CP	EH	HS	HF TC	MHB	SP
269. God of concrete, God of steel	33					23			
270. God of grace and God of glory	34		372	563		24	324		
271. God of love and truth and beauty	35								
272. God of mercy, God of grace		264	373	330	395		293	681	170
273. Guide me, O thou great Redeemer		296	541	500	397		528	615	508
274. Hail to the Lord's anointed!		219	80	326	45		190	245	87
275. Help us, O Lord, to learn	40						493		
276. Immortal, invisible, God only wise		372	61	28	407		21	34	535
277. Jesus calls us! o'er the tumult		533	416	451	205		104	157	217
278. Jesus shall reign where'er the sun		220	184	158	420		516	272	545
279. Jesus, where'er thy people meet		245	338	266	422		371	675	551
280. Judge eternal, throned in splendour			643	572	423		329	883	552
281. Lead us, heavenly Father, lead us		311	43	507	426		525	611	555
282. Let all the world in every corner sing		375	13	3	427		342	5	556
283. Let creation bless the Father							312		
284. Lord as we rise to leave this shell	52								
285. Lord God, by whom all change is wrought				60				55	
286. Lord Jesus Christ	58					86	417		

		AHH FT	AMR	BHB	CP	EH	HS	HF TC	MHB	SP
287.	Lord Jesus, once you spoke to man	59								
288.	Lord, look upon our working days						87	112		
289.	Lord of all hopefulness	61		631	534			101		565
290.	Lord of all power	62						547		
291.	Lord of lords and King Eternal	63								
292.	Lord, thy church						42			
293.	Love divine, all loves excelling		205	595	179	437		217	431	573
294.	Now let us from this table rise	70					50	419		
295.	Now thank we all our God		379	18	42	533		33	10	350
296.	O God of Bethel		299	550	55	447		35	607	596
297.	O God of earth and altar				578	562				308
298.	O God of truth, whose living word		309	517	522	449				597
299.	O God our help in ages past				52			37		598
300.	O God you give to all mankind							313		
301.	O Jesus, I have promised		331	298	447	577		531	526	255
302.	O Lord of every shining constellation	78						314		
303.	O Loving Lord, who art for ever seeking			602					577	
304.	O praise ye the Lord		376		25			354		351
305.	O worship the King		167	22	17	466		24	8	618
306.	O worship the Lord		77	35	275			344	9	93

	AHH FT	AMR	BHB	CP	EH	HS	HF TC	MHB	SP
307. Praise and thanksgiving	82								
308. Praise my soul		365	23	18	470		38	12	623
309. Praise, O praise our God and King		481						19	
310. Praise the Lord!		368	24	13	535		583	13	624
311. Praise to the Holiest in the heights		185	216	71	471		140	74	625
312. Praise to the Lord		382	25	45	536		40	64	626
313. Put thou thy trust in God		310							
314. Rejoice, O land, in God thy might		582	651	571	475		331	882	631
315. Rejoice, the Lord is King		216	190	161	476		180	247	632
316. Servant of all, to toil for man	86								
317. Sing we a song of high revolt			632					575	
318. Son of God, eternal Saviour		207	652	558	529		102		339
319. Stand up, and bless the Lord		374	363	270			351	685	
320. Teach me, my God and King	89	337	487	433	485			597	652
321. Tell out, my soul, the greatness of the Lord							42		
322. The earth, O Lord, is one great field		472			168				
323. The Lord will come and not be slow		52	195	156	492			813	658
324. The sower went forth sowing		486							
325. Thy hand, O God, has guided		256	264	251	545		536		

	AHH FT	AMR	BHB	CP	EH	HS	HF TC	MHB	SP
326. Thy kingdom come, O God		262	397	584	554		334	811	680
327. To Thee, O Lord, our hearts we raise		484	731	649				964	13
328. We find thee Lord in others' needs	97								
329. We have a gospel to proclaim	98								
330. Were you there when they crucified my Lord						93	519		
331. We turn to you						73			
332. What does the Lord require	99								
333. When I needed a neighbour	100					97			

Key to hymnbook abbreviations

AHHFT	A Hundred Hymns for Today	HS	Hymns and Songs
AMR	Ancient and Modern Revised	HFTC	Hymns For Today's Church
BHB	Baptist Hymn Book	MHB	Methodist Hymn Book
CP	Congregational Praise	SP	Songs of Praise
EH	English Hymnal		

(b) Hymns not found in the selection of hymnbooks

334.   Glory be to Thee, O God, Hallelujah,
Father, Son and Holy Ghost, Hallelujah.

God is working in our day, Hallelujah,
We can see his mighty deeds, Hallelujah.

We can see Him in our town, Hallelujah,
Calling men to live as men, Hallelujah.

God is present where men live, Hallelujah,
In the colonies and slums, Hallelujah.

God is present where men work, Hallelujah,
In the factories and mills, Hallelujah.

God is present where men learn, Hallelujah,
In the colleges and schools, Hallelujah.

God is present where men play, Hallelujah,
In the cinema and sports, Hallelujah.

God is there where man's oppressed, Hallelujah,
Calling him to humanness, Hallelujah.

God is there where men decide, Hallelujah,
Calling them to choose the good, Hallelujah.

God is present everywhere, Hallelujah,
In man's weakness and his strength, Hallelujah.

God is working in our day, Hallelujah,
Loving, judging, setting free, Hallelujah.

WHERE WE SEE OUR GOD AT WORK, HALLE-
LUJAH,
THERE SHALL WE, HIS PEOPLE, BE, HALLE-
LUJAH.

335.   God of fire and wind and water,
Lord of forge and lamp and flame;
Welder of the mightiest matter
In earth's lofty molten frame.
Earth's abysses own thy vigour,
Heaven's recesses blaze thy fires,
Mountains fused to timeless rigour
Own they serve Thy high desires.

Thou the Lord of all things living
Hast not left us without guide;
Torn by passions, fears and weakness,
(Small our bark, the seas how wide!)
Praise to Thee whose mind far-reaching
Sent the Carpenter to dwell
Here on earth with heavenly teaching
How to love and serve Thee well.

He who once on earth a workman
Sharpened tool and shaped the wood,
And with manual toil and labour
Tried Thy works and proved them good;
Him we serve, from Thee descended,
Son of God and Son of Man,
Who by earthly chance attended
Trod the path of Everyman.

Thine, O God, the deep invention
Of the arts our strength employs,
And Thy wisdom hath created
Ores and metals and alloys.
Teach us how to use Thy treasures
For the betterment of life,
Till we turn to peaceful measures
All the implements of strife.

336.   God is unique and one –
Father, Sustainer, Lord!
Patterns of life were spun

by his creative Word.
Of his intention, love and care
we are with growing trust aware.

Love came to earth in Christ
Our common life to share;
choosing to be the least,
willing a cross to bear.
He died, he rose, that we might live
and all our love, responding, give.

The Holy Spirit moves
man to discover man;
his inspiration proves
more than the mind can span.
Each listening heart is led to find
the will of God for all mankind.

He shall for ever reign,
ruler of time and space;
God in the midst, alive,
seen in the human face.
We give expression to our creed
by love in thought, in word and deed.

337.   Great God of Town and City
We offer praise to you,
From House and Flat and Sitter
Our thanks we bring to you.
With varied feelings merging
In one great song of praise,
Glad, now we stand before you,
Hear, God, the hymn we raise.

You are the God of business,
Of commerce and of art,
Of industry and law court,
Of college and of sport;
Your purpose still is working

In spite of slum and shame,
The purpose that will lead men
To glorify your name.

You are the God of music,
Of hospital and home,
Of factory and Town Hall,
Of parkland where we roam;
Your judgement is on all things,
On pride and cruel deed,
On those who exploit others,
On those so deaf to need.

Great God of this great city,
In song we offer praise;
We see your love in action
In many varied ways,
Your purpose still excites us,
Your judgement helps us plan,
How we can make this city
A brotherhood of man.

338.   In quest for knowledge, truth and skill
We trace a great creator's will;
In mill and market, school and street,
The ground is holy where we meet.

In workshop sounds, in engines strong,
We hear an echo of his song:
On dock and building site, in mine
True work fulfils a scheme divine.

New ways of healing now he shows;
Through caring hands God's blessing flows;
His science aids the farmer's toil
As food springs forth from fertile soil.

Across the world we greet our friends;
Nation to nation wealth extends;

Ships soar in space its realms to scan;
Calls from the stars are heard by man.

Atom and Universe proclaim
The source of life our lips can name;
We, who his greater glory share
Will by our lives his love declare.

339. Lord, for the years your love has kept and guided,
Urged and inspired us, cheered us on our way;
Sought us and saved us, pardoned and provided,
Lord of the years, we bring our thanks today.

Lord, for your Word, the Word of life which fires us,
Speaks to our hearts and sets our souls ablaze;
Teaches and trains, rebukes us and inspires us,
Lord of the Word, receive your people's praise.

Lord, for our land, in this our generation,
Spirits oppressed by pleasure, wealth and care;
For young and old, for commonwealth and nation,
Lord of our land, be pleased to hear our prayer.

Lord, for our world, when we disown and doubt him,
Loveless in strength and comfortless in pain;
Hungry and helpless, lost indeed without him,
Lord of the world, we pray that Christ may reign.

Lord, for ourselves; in living power remake us –
Self on the cross and Christ upon the throne –
Past put behind us, for the future take us,
Lord of our lives, to live for Christ alone.

340. Lord God, in whom all worlds,
All life, all work, began:
Give us faith to know
We serve your master plan.
How happy they who thus have found
Contentment in the daily round.

But when good work receives
No adequate reward;
When meaningless routines
Leave willing workers bored;
When time is spent in needless strife;
Make us ashamed, O Lord of life.

And if, in leaner years,
What we have gained is lost;
If progress must be bought
At someone else's cost:
Make us, one nation, swift to share
The hardships others have to bear.

So, for tomorrow's sake
Teach us new skills today,
To do your perfect will
In our imperfect way,
And live as those whom you have called
To be your work-force in the world.

341.   O Lord, we can't see you, Oh help us to know
That you are still here, as you said.
'I'm here,' says the Lord, 'to the end of the world,
Though people may say I am dead,' he says,
'Though people may say I am dead.'

'I'm cold,' says the Lord, 'I am frightened and
   scorned;
With the prisoner in jail there I'll be;
I am old and I'm lonely; I'm young and unloved;
Just look and you'll surely find me,' he says,
'Just look and you'll surely find me.'

'I live in a slum, I sleep on a bench,
I am dumb, I am deaf, I can't see.
I haven't a job and I haven't a home,
But there's few that take pity on me,' he says,
'There's few that take pity on me.'

'I'm with every man in his life, in his work,
For I'm worker and boss just the same.
I'm Trades' Union member; I'm strike breaker too,
For to be with my brothers I came,' he says,
'To be with my brothers I came.'

'I'm Vietnamese, and American too,
I am Arab Guerilla and Jew.
I'm Tory and Labour, I'm black and I'm white,
For I'm all men if only you knew,' he says,
'I'm all men if only you knew.'

'You scourge and you crucify me with your wars:
With the wounded and maimed I share pain.
In riots I'm beaten, by murderers killed,
But you leave me to die there again, my sons,
You leave me to die there again.'

O Lord, is it we who don't see you in need,
Who leave you in want and despair?
'My sons, in the world there is strife and much pain,
Go out and you'll find that I'm there,' he says,
'Go out and you'll find that I'm there.'

342.   Our song is of the city where alone man can be free,
Free from slavery and prejudice and immaturity;
Free to build his own tomorrows with the vision he
   can see
Of the dignity of man.

Chorus: Men of Christ, we work together,
             Men of Christ, we work together,
             Men of Christ, we work together,
             For the dignity of man.

Deep within our city's people, marred by bitterness
   and pain
By long years of degradation, of injustice, fear and
   shame,

Burns the light of our humanity, that strong persistent
    flame
Of the dignity of man.

Chorus: Men of Christ . . .

For our city with its power, and our city with its
pride,
With its grime and with its glory and its freedom to
    decide:
Is the place where God is living and the place for
    which He died;
The city of our God.

Chorus: Men of Christ, we strive together,
            Men of Christ, we strive together,
            Building in His Power together
            The city of Our God.

343.   Sing we of the modern city,
        scene alike of joy and stress;
        sing we of its nameless people
        in their urban wilderness.
        Into endless rows of houses
        life is set a million-fold,
        life expressed in human beings
        daily born and growing old.

        In the city full of people,
        world of speed and hectic days;
        in the ever-changing setting
        of the latest trend and craze,
        Christ is present, and among us,
        in the crowd, we see him stand.
        In the bustle of the city
        Jesus Christ is Everyman.

        God is not remote in heaven
        but on earth to share our shape;

changing graph and mass and numbers
into persons with a name.
Christ has shown, beyond statistics,
human life with glory crowned;
by his timeless presence proving
people matter, people count!

344.   Surrounded by a world of need,
by cries for healing, housing, bread,
our mind is given to despair,
and hope is undermined by war.

Yet through the fabric of our time
there runs the liberating theme
of love that makes the world go round,
of love creative and profound.

This love is in the face of Christ,
in human life, made manifest;
its strong intent will conquer all,
it raises people when they fall.

Then help us Lord, to understand
the claims and blessings of your plan,
and use, to bring your reign about,
those in the church and those without.

345.   The earth, the sky, the oceans
and all that they contain;
the world with all its secrets,
it is the Lord's domain.
To rule his great creation,
God has endowed mankind
with gifts of strength and courage
and an inventive mind.

For quest and exploration,
Our God has given the key

to free the hidden forces
and wealth of soil and sea.
To new advance in science,
research to conquer pain,
to growth in skill and knowledge
we are by God ordained.

To us from birth is given
our stewardship and brief:
to search for truth and purpose,
to find the heart of life.
God calls us to adventure
with work of hand and brain;
to share with all his people
the profits we may gain.

We pledge ourselves to service,
that with the help of Christ
we may be able stewards
of all that does exist.
Whate'er we may discover,
on earth, in outer space,
God grant that we may use it
to bless the human race.

346. The fathers built this city – In ages long ago,
       And busy in its busy streets – They hurried to and
           fro.
       The children played around them – And sang the
           songs of yore,
       Till, one by one, they fell asleep – To work and play
           no more.

       Yet still the city standeth – A hive of toiling men,
       And mother love makes happy home – For children
           now as then;
       O God of ages, help us – Such citizens to be,
       That children's children here may sing – The songs of
           liberty.

Let all the people praise Thee – Give all Thy saving
  health,
Or vain the labourer's strong right arm – And vain
  the merchant's wealth;
Send forth Thy light to 'stablish – The glory of the
  Word,
Until this city is become – The city of the Lord.

A commonweal of brothers – United, great and
  small,
Upon our banner blazoned be – The Charter, 'Each
  for all!'
Nor let us cease from battle – Nor weary sheath the
  sword,
Until this city is become – The city of the Lord.

347.   The harvest of the city
We lift to you today,
Who call us all to celebrate,
To labour and to play.
You only are the maker
In all we make and do,
You share with us the labour,
You share the music too.

> Holy is the maker
> Who lives in all we do
> And holy is the liberty
> To be a maker too.

We share with you the river,
We share with you the road,
The driving of the lorry and
The lifting of the load.
We share with you the timber,
We share with you the steel,
The lifting of the hammer,
The turning of the wheel.

Holy is the maker . . .

In hospital and harbour
We meet you night and day.
We share with you the writing and
The acting of a play.
We find you in the teaching
And in the learning too.
In all that we are making
You are the maker too.

Holy is the maker . . .

The harvest of the city
We bring to you today,
And by the liberty you give
We celebrate and play.
You only are the maker,
You live in all we do.
We share with you the labour,
We share the music too.

Holy is the maker . . .

348.   When through the whirl of wheels, and engines
      humming,
Patient in power for the sons of men,
Peals like a trumpet promise of His coming
Who in the clouds is pledged to come again;

When through the night the furnace fires flaring,
Loud with their tongues of flame like spurting blood,
Speak to the heart of love, alive and daring,
Sing of the boundless energy of God;

When in the depths the patient miner striving,
Feels in his arms the vigour of the Lord,
Strikes for a kingdom and his King's arriving,
Holding his pick more splendid than the sword;

When on the sweat of labour and its sorrow,
Toiling in twilight, flickering and dim,
Flames out the sunshine of the great tomorrow,
When all the world looks up – because of Him.

Then will He come – with meekness for His glory,
God in a workman's jacket as before,
Living again the eternal Gospel story,
Sweeping the shavings from His workshop floor.

(c) Psalms

349. Ps.8   Man has a special destiny and re-
                               sponsibility.

350. Ps.15   The honest man is acceptable to God
                               and obeys his laws.

351. Ps.19   God's creation bears witness to the
                               plan and design of the world.

352. Ps.46   In times of trouble God is our
                               strength and help.

353. Ps.65   God has ordered the world and has
                               given man enough to supply his
                               needs.

354. Ps.67   God has blessed mankind.

355. Ps.90   God sees man's misuse of his crea-
                               tion.

356. Ps.95   God is our creator and our salvation.
                               Let us give thanks.

357. Ps.96   Give thanks to God for his creation.

358.   Ps.100   Rejoice for all that God has done.

359.   Ps.104:1–25   God's creation is vast and his many
                          works are glorious.

360.   Ps.107:23–32   God is active in his creation.

(d) Hymns and songs suggested for various subjects

(i) Confession

See items numbered 244, 256, 258.

(ii) Commitment

See items numbered 259, 266, 286, 287 and 301.

(iii) Creation

See items numbered 267, 268, 269, 289, 302, 325, 335, 336, 347, 349 and 351.

(iv) Creative work

See items numbered 245, 253, 288, 316 and 338.

(v) Dedication

See items numbered 239, 260, 262, 281, 294 and 344.

(vi) **Praise**

See items numbered 238, 254, 263, 271, 282, 283, 304, 306, 307 and 321.

(vii) **Service**

See items numbered 241, 270, 275, 277, 284, 290, 292, 303, 328, 340, 341 and 345.

(viii) **Thanksgiving**

See items numbered 264, 295, 334, 337, 339, 357 and 358.

(ix) **Visions of the Kingdom**

See items numbered 237, 252, 265, 291, 317, 326, 342, 343, 346 and 348.

UNEMPLOYMENT

(a) Prayers
(b) Litanies
(c) Readings: biblical
(d) Readings: non-biblical
(e) Sentences
(f) Hymns and songs

UNEMPLOYMENT

(a) Prayers

361. O God, the Creator of all things, you made men in your own image to seek joy in creative work. Have mercy on all who are unemployed, and help us so to order our common life that everyone may have work to do and find joy in doing it, to the good of this nation and to the glory of your name; through Jesus Christ our Lord. Amen.

362. O Lord Jesus Christ, you were lifted up on the cross to draw all people into unity with yourself.

Look in mercy upon this nation divided by unemployment,
Send out your light and your faith that they may lead us along the paths of fellowship and peace.

Help us to share with each other, work with each other, and learn from one another, that we may live in unity together, to your glory and the welfare of everyone, for your name's sake. Amen.

363. O God, you have called all men to co-operate with you in the work of your creation and you require of men that they glorify you in their labour: look in your mercy on those who are denied the opportunity of work at this time. Save their hearts from bitterness and their souls from hopelessness, and hasten the time when they may be called again to join the ranks of their fellow-workers.

Stir our consciences, O God, and kindle our imaginations that we may never accept the scandal of their

present predicament. And so strengthen our wills that
we persevere in seeking a more just ordering of social
life, that all may be given the opportunity to serve
you and one another in brotherhood and goodwill.
Amen.

364.   O God, be with our leaders as they plan our futures and
shape our lives. Soften their hearts to help those who
are denied the fulfilment of work, that the quality of
life of all the people of this nation may be seen as more
important than pure finance.

Never let us see the 'unemployed' in terms of a label
or as just numbers on a sheet. Help us to understand
the appalling tragedy of lives lived with no meaning, of
lives lived without hope, of dreams shattered and of
families torn apart. Pour down your Holy Spirit to heal
these broken lives and we pray, that strengthened by
the same spirit, we may bring hope to those in despair.

We ask this through your Son, Jesus Christ our Lord,
who brought the victory of light over darkness to your
sinful world, and to whom with You and the Holy Spirit
we give praise and thanksgiving. Amen.

365.   Lord God, who in Jesus was a friend to those who were
cast out by society, hold on to those who feel rejected
today. Be with them in their despair, helplessness and
fear. That they may come to know you as always
present with the victims of the suffering of the world
and find hope in you. We ask this through the one who
suffered and died, and in the power of the One who
gives true life to all. Amen.

366.   Help me today, Lord.
Help me to get through the day.
Help me to remember those who love me.
Help me not to give up hope.
Help me to get moving again.
Lord, help me. Amen.

(b) Litanies

367. For our failure to understand the needs of people who are out of work.
Lord have mercy.
For our reluctance to share what we have with those in need.
Christ have mercy.
For our complacency in not working to create a more just society.
Lord have mercy.

368. We pray for the unemployed, particularly those in our parish and neighbourhood, that they may retain their sense of dignity and value.
Lord hear our prayer.   *Lord in your mercy hear us.*

We pray especially for young people who are without work. Help them not to feel rejected and unwanted and to discover ways of playing a useful and positive role in the community.
Lord hear our prayer.   *Lord in your mercy hear us.*

We pray for fathers of families who have been made redundant. Help them to retain the respect of their family.
Lord hear our prayer.   *Lord in your mercy hear us.*

We pray for Politicians, Employers, Trade Union Leaders, and all those who are involved in decisions which could create more jobs. Give them guidance and fill them with compassion so that their decisions will be in the best interests of the community.
Lord hear our prayer.   *Lord in your mercy hear us.*

Lord, watch over us your children. Give us the strength and wisdom to find effective solutions to the new problems we face. Help us to discover new opportunities of serving you and each other. Fill us with hope so

that we can bring your love and compassion to those
who are in danger of despair.
Lord hear our prayer.   *Lord in your mercy hear us.*

369.   Lord God, be with our brothers and sisters who are
without work.
We ask that they may be given
- hope in their hopelessness
- courage instead of fear
- peace to replace anxiety
- confidence in place of doubt
- energy to overcome listlessness
- and determination which replaces resentment.

Lord hear us   *Lord, let your love come to be with
them*

May we who have jobs
- never patronise those without work
- never write them off
- never think we are better or more important
- and never think that material things are more
important than people.

Lord hear us   *Lord, let us love them*

Heal our divided nation, Lord, through your Holy
Spirit. Bring together
- north and south
- the employed and unemployed
- the rural and the urban
- the rich and those on social security.

Bind us together through your love to create a nation
worthy of your Kingdom.

Lord hear us   *Lord, let your love be with us all, to
bind us together. Amen.*

370.   Lord God Almighty, we pray for those without work,
- for young people who have left school and who have
never had the chance to understand the fulfilment of
creative work,

Lord in your mercy   *Hear our prayer*

– for older men with families who have lost the security and focus of their lives,

Lord in your mercy *Hear our prayer*

– for skilled men put out of work, be with them in their frustration at not being able to use their talents,

Lord in your mercy *Hear our prayer*

– for those who had positions of responsibility, who have now lost their status, help them to use their abilities and not to become disillusioned,

Lord in your mercy *Hear our prayer*

– for self-employed men and women who have had their businesses destroyed by the fluctuations of economic forces, strengthen them not to lose the will to create and build,

Lord in your mercy *Hear our prayer*

– for the families of those unemployed, that they may be strengthened in their support of their brothers and sisters, mothers and fathers, sons and daughters, help them to grow together and not to be ripped apart by despair,

Lord in your mercy *Hear our prayer*

– for those who are alone, those who are unemployed who have no one with whom to share their fears, send your Spirit to be with them,

Lord in your mercy *Hear our prayer*

– for those who will never work again, those who have no hope, do not let them lose their self-respect, support them and help them to use their abilities wherever they can,

Lord in your mercy *Hear our prayer*

Be with the unemployed of our country, Lord, no one is unimportant to you, no one is unloved by you, carry them in your love, maintain their dreams and bring them to fulfilment in their lives. We ask these petitions in the knowledge of your love shown to the world through your Son, Jesus Christ our Lord. *Amen.*

(c) Readings: biblical

The following section lists references to biblical readings with a summary of their content only, rather than the full Bible texts themselves.

371.   ISAIAH 58:7–10
To serve God is to serve those in need, for through us God can bring those in darkness to light.

372.   JEREMIAH 31:31–34
God can redeem any situation. Through his love everything can be made new.

373.   LAMENTATIONS 3:19–33
Even in the darkest hour, have faith in God, for hope is to be found in his love.

374.   HOSEA 14:1,2,4–7
God is loving; he will care for us even when those around reject us.

375.   AMOS 5:4,5,10–13
God is just. He seeks truth and judges people not by what they have but by what they are.

376.   MARK 14:22–31,34–39
God himself suffered for us. God is present in our suffering. He gives us hope in our troubles and will redeem us.

377.   LUKE 10:25–37
The parable of the Good Samaritan reminds us that we are to care for those whom the world rejects.

378. LUKE 15:3–10
No one is ever lost from the sight of God. Those who seem alone are loved by God.

379. ACTS 2:42–47
The fellowship of Christians is wide enough to embrace all those in need. The way we live shows our concern for them and the Gospel.

380. ROMANS 12:14–21
Suffering causes bitterness, but bitterness destroys its victim. Look to God; have hope in him for the future.

(d) Readings: non-biblical

Adding insult to injury?

381. It appears that some firms have made people redundant and required them to leave immediately, in some cases with no more than a few hours notice. Some of these employees have been with their companies many years. Of course they will receive their redundancy entitlements and the statutory 90 days pay and in some cases extra payment on top. But is this really the way to treat people however necessary it is for the redundancy itself? No time for farewells let alone a leaving party, scarcely time apparently to gather their things and pack up.

It implies that people have no other commitment to a company but as a source of earning money and that they are regarded as merely tools of the business to be dispensed with at a moment's notice when no longer required. There are many more things about being employed than the money to be earned from it. An office or section is by way of being a community to which people belong and which gives some meaning and purpose to life, even for those who find their actual work uncongenial. This kind of treatment both for the dismissed and for those who remain is a violent dismemberment. It cannot do other than engender the feeling that employees are just things, merely functions in the productive process and no more. How on earth can a company expect its employees to feel any sense of commitment and loyalty to the enterprise when they know that they can be dispensed with at the drop of a hat?

My last day

382.   Sadly I walk through gates of th'owd mill,
Dejected in spirit, no soul with a will.
Thrown ont' scrap heap, a worn out part,
Only to finish, last day with no heart.

Friendship was made as we worked side by side,
Proud of our work we shared with such pride.
We had faults, as all workmates will say,
Forgiven, forgotten, on this the last day.

Shared our secrets of heartaches and fears,
A big loving family with eyes full of tears.
Memories will linger, some pass away,
Sadly I walk on this the last day.

Shamelessly crying, I meet the day's end,
Clasping a hand of workmate and friend.
Knowing so well, those days I will miss,
Saddened to part, wi' nowt but a kiss.

Having to lose all friends on the floor,
Sadly I walk through t'little red door.
Lost are the days we laughed or cried,
To miss my mates, last day, mill died.

Not wanted

383. There's nothing like 'finding a formula' for concealing a disagreeable truth. And if you can't find a formula – which in some mysterious way, lifts the liability from oneself for action – then find an impressive-sounding word. 'Redundancy' is one of these. It sounds better than 'unemployment' – and somehow suggests that we aren't right back in the old black days of queues at the Exchange.

But whatever you call it, the harsh fact remains that, at this moment of writing, men and women are without a job.

What does this mean for the person concerned? Above and beyond the mere economics – or perhaps, far below and more deeply, if unconsciously, felt – are the human and psychological aspects of 'redundancy'.

Take, for example, three groups out of those affected. First, the school-leavers. These are the young people whom we accuse of being 'anti-social' and 'irresponsible'. We send them out from schools where they've at least learned something of mutual responsibility, have seen something of what good work can be, have had their time occupied and their maintenance assured.

They find themselves rejected by the world they are longing to enter. The day is an endless stretch to be somehow filled in – and there's no money for all the ways in which it could be filled.

Second, the elderly unskilled labourer or semi-skilled machine-minder. This figure is one of the tragedies of our society. He has never had the opportunity – perhaps has shown little inclination – for qualifying with any degree of craftsmanship.

And now he's out of a job. All his security is gone. He's not the sort of person to find it easy to re-train or to move his household to an area of greater employment. He has believed that if you kept good time, put in a fair day's work, and paid your union sub, you'd never be on the street. Now he is. And he feels disgraced, less than a man.

Third, the skilled craftsman. He may be unemployed because of the general slump – or because his particular qualification, laboriously obtained over the years, is no longer wanted. The latter is perhaps the saddest form of 'redundancy'. Here is a man who, with sacrifice of time and effort, has obtained skills which have promoted him to the elite of industry. Now they've suddenly become a drug on the market. He sees teenage girls tending machines which do everything he used to do – and very much faster. Are you going to sap his pride in himself, his human dignity, still further by pushing him down into the semi-skilled?

If industry is simply our people at work, using our collective resources for our common good and their own individual satisfaction, then for us to allow the waste and inefficiency of 'redundancy' is for us to prove unworthy of our past freedom and present hopes. 'Unemployment' is neither an unpredictable natural calamity nor yet an inevitable part of organised industry; it is simply the symptom of our collective inertia in the face of immediate challenge.

People and the economy

384. We face, at the moment, a chronic mismatch between the needs of human beings and the pressures exerted by our economic system. This system of production, distribution and consumption has become so complex and inter-related as to demand that the whole of our national culture be organised around it. If we allow this process to continue, then as Robert Theobald predicted in 1965, 'the economic system will increasingly become a parasite on the total environment, depriving the men who create it of their psychological and social sustenance and, in return, providing them with only economic gains.'

I wonder if this process is not already well advanced?

In the sort of bewildering change we are experiencing at present, we need to remind ourselves, loud and clear, that we are not just units of the economy, we are people. When the Bishop of Coventry told the marchers on the People's March for Jobs: 'We are not here to serve economic systems, they are here to serve us,' not only was he loudly applauded but he was echoing the words of Jesus, who said: 'The sabbath was made for the sake of man, and not man for the sabbath.'

Such statements seek to restore a proper value perspective, and remind us that when any man-made system, whether economic, political or religious, ceases to respond adequately to the changing needs and aspirations of people it becomes burdensome and oppressive.

I am not trying to create new slogans but to draw attention to two underlying issues. First, that what is happening to us at present cannot be adequately explained simply by reference to the 'economy'. In recent years that bad-tempered 'god' has come to dominate our lives, and every twitch of his eyebrows, faithfully studied and reported obsessively by the media. Economic policies alone are not a sufficient response. Secondly, when, as they say, 'the economy picks up again', we shall not be where we were before but somewhere 'new'. For quite a while now, Britain has been fermenting new wine and, to quote Jesus again, 'new wine requires new bottles.'

We must not under-estimate the far-reaching nature of current social change. It is not just the economy that is changing but also our human and social values. Assumptions about the dignity and value of human beings and the place of justice and equality in their relationships have been changing and are now looking for appropriate structures through which to express themselves.

If the economy is to be our servant, not our god, then

it must embody and enable those human values, goals and relationships, which our community is now seeking to pursue.

Social and psychological well-being

385. One of the cruellest effects of prolonged unemployment is that the individuals concerned tend to blame themselves for their predicament. Numerous studies have documented the demoralisation, loss of self-respect and self-confidence experienced by those who are without work for a long period.

Being unemployed is very different from having leisure time. The unemployed decrease their attendance at clubs and voluntary organisations, their use of libraries and the amount they read. This is no doubt partly a consequence of poverty and demoralisation, and partly of their shame at being without work.

There are some exceptions to the general picture of apathy and resignation. Louis Harris, the American pollster, found that high unemployment amongst young blacks in northern cities in the USA was correlated with support for radical and revolutionary ideas. Pre-war studies of unemployment and criminal activity show a connection between delinquency and unemployment.

Lengthy unemployment affects family relationships and leads to argument, conflict and, in some cases, violence and family breakdown. The NSPCC has recently expressed fears about the likely increase in child-battering as unemployment increases.

There is evidence of a series of phases in the reaction of individuals to the experience of unemployment; there is an immediate shock effect, followed by a period of intense activity and active job search, but finally despair and apathy. A MSC study showed that many of the long-term unemployed had become very pessimistic about finding work, and found it difficult to sustain job-seeking activity in the face of continued rejection and failure. All were unhappy about their situation and badly wanted the opportunity to work again.

Social costs of unemployment

386. In 1976 Professor Harvey Brenner was commissioned by the Joint Economic Committee of the US Congress to conduct a wide-ranging study into the social costs of unemployment and evaluate these in financial terms. Senator Hubert Humphrey in his preface to Brenner's report concluded that 'the 1.4 per cent rise in unemployment during 1970 has cost our society nearly 7 billion dollars lost income due to illness, mortality, and in added state prison and mental hospital outlays. To this must be added public outlays of some 2.8 billion dollars annually over the 1970–1975 period for jobless and welfare payments.'

Following this report Brenner was asked to conduct a similar study in England. Brenner focused initially on Liverpool and Nottingham and (although sceptical at first because of the presence of a welfare system free on demand) he found exactly the same correlation between unemployment and the levels of mortality and morbidity for both those cities, and for England and Wales as a whole, as he had done in the USA. Using the formulae developed by Brenner, a recent social accounting exercise by a team from the University of Cambridge into the ramifications of closing down steel-making in Corby have found that a sustained rise in unemployment of one million could, over a five-year period in the UK, lead to something like 50,000 more deaths, over 60,000 additional cases of mental illness and 14,000 more receiving prison sentences. In terms of financial implications these social costs would give rise to heavy additional public expenditure on law and order and £280 million on health and community services over a five-year period.

Unemployment is not evenly spread throughout the population. Therefore, these costs are disproportionately borne by certain sections within society. The financial costs of unemployment are, especially in the early stages of unemployment, very high to the government. Although not enough research has yet been carried out into the social costs of unemployment and what exists is not entirely conclusive, there is enough evidence to suggest that unemployment psychologically and physiologically damages the individual. Many others apart from the unemployed person may also be affected. Hence, if these costs are added to the more obvious financial costs, there would seem to be a strong case for arguing that unemployment is a major and very costly social disease.

The Christian truth

387. The conflict between human and physical realities on the one hand and economic and financial practice on the other (between the facts of abundance and an induced scarcity), has an important religious significance. In the first place, our present arrangements virtually condemn man to regard economic activity as his chief end. However successful he has been in providing for his wants and saving himself trouble, he must keep on keeping on, making work as a condition of enjoying the combined fruits of the earth and human skill. Those who cannot remain in the treadmill are thrown out and crushed.

In the second place, while the Church must recognise the autonomy of secular discipline, she is not called upon to refrain from proclaiming that a religious and moral obligation rests upon men to make economic and monetary practice reflect economic realities. Where there is every physical and human facility for a particular human purpose, as there has been in the modern world for some generations for a vast relaxation of economic activity, no 'laws' of economics or money which imply its impossibility can rightly escape the judgement, made in the name of religion, that they violate truth.

It even looks today as if the moralising of the world and its appeal to religion really is a request that whatever influence religion may retain should be exercised in persuading men to accept an artificial strait-jacket of economy, from which the world has derived its habits and theories. One of the tasks of the Church is to demand in the name of truth that these theories and habits be radically re-considered, for Christ is the Truth as well as the Way and the Life. The message of religion for the present economic plight of the world must be based on the axiom that the end of economic activities and of all economic implements, like money, trade and employment, is use and enjoyment. We work to live rather than live to work, and life for the Christian includes so much more than secular activity.

The end of a work-based society?

388. Our 'new unemployment' arises because industry can be more efficient because it operates with fewer people. Examples from oil, petrochemicals, telecommunications and ship-building illustrate this. But redundancy is resisted in the name of human dignity. I want to question this assumption that a man in losing his job loses all his dignity. Many jobs diminish people and only seem attractive if they are about to be lost. Also there are many people, and whole ancient and Christian traditions, where dignity is to be found outside paid employment. The Protestant work-ethic should be challenged. 'Work', as creative purposeful activity involving the taking and shaping of natural resources with a view to enhancing human well-being, need not be the same thing as 'paid employment'. Some people 'work' harder in their leisure-time pursuits than in their paid employment. Other things than work are necessary to human dignity. 'Doing' must be complemented by 'being' in rest, contemplation and spiritual regeneration. Most people have lost the capacity for leisure, and enforced leisure feels like sloth. The present trend towards automation contains an element of promise. A new consciousness must be engineered, especially for young people, in which work and leisure receive new definition.

Unemployment as someone else's problem

389. I detect a rather disturbing symptom of tribalism in the way in which those who still have jobs sometimes seem to close ranks all too quickly against those who have lost them. I don't mean that we are not concerned about unemployment in general, nor that we fail to do our utmost to preserve jobs. But once people actually become unemployed they seem to drop out into a kind of no-man's land. They disappear from the various structures and interest groups and centres of power, which might otherwise continue to give them a voice within the industrial system, rather than outside it. So the only voice left to them becomes the mass voice of marchers, which can only make a noise without actually negotiating anything. The kind of hard bargaining which ought to be going on at all levels inside particular industries and unions, in the places where actual decisions about new jobs and job-sharing might be made, doesn't seem to happen. The problem is projected outside the structures to become 'the general problem of unemployment'.

Unemployment is unacceptable

390.   At the outset it seems perfectly clear that 'work is for man' and not 'man is for work.' This is of the greatest possible importance because it means that the essential value of work – of all work – is man himself; and it is this fact that gives work its true dignity rather than an evaluation of the consequences of the work. This is one of the principal points made by Pope John Paul in his Encyclical 'On Human Work'. I cannot do better than quote two sentences from that remarkable treatise of Catholic teaching:

'This circumstance (the One who, while being God, became like us in all things, devoted most of his life on earth to manual work at the carpenter's bench) constitutes in itself the most eloquent "Gospel of work", showing that the basis for determining the value of human work is not primarily the kind of work being done but the fact that the one who is doing it is a person. The sources of the dignity of work are to be sought primarily in the subjective dimension, not in the objective one.'

From this I believe that it logically follows that because in essential value all men are equal, therefore all work is to be seen as of equal value and the whole 'class structure of work' must be rejected as positively as we reject the notion of a hierarchy of classes of human beings, and all the other false values of materialism and economism which elevate the objective value of work and treat people as 'instruments of production' whose labour is to be bought and sold like any other piece of merchandise. Man is called to have dominion over the earth and it is by means of work that this is achieved. If it is true that by doing God's will and obeying his commandments we become more human in the process, then work is an important factor in the development of our humanity. This surely is the experience of the great majority of people. No matter how irksome unpleasant work may sometimes seem,

there is in the long run an internal sense of fulfilment
that we enjoy; and when we are prevented from working there is a great sense of deprivation. I believe this is
a vitally important observation at this present time
when so many millions are denied the opportunity
which most of us enjoy to engage in normal paid
employment. It is an affront to our humanity and an
evil which must not be allowed to persist. From a
Christian perspective involuntary unemployment is, I
consider, unacceptable.

(e) Sentences

391. The steadfast love of the Lord never ceases, his mercies
never come to an end, they are new every morning;
great is thy faithfulness. (Lam. 3:22–23)

392. Enter by the narrow gate; for the gate is wide and the
way is easy, that leads to destruction, and those who
enter by it are many. For the gate is narrow and the way
is hard, that leads to life, and those who find it are few.
(Matt. 7:13–14)

393. Lord, when did we see you hungry or thirsty or a
stranger or naked or sick or in prison and did not
minister to you? (Matt. 25:44)

394. He who is least among you all is the one who is great.
(Luke 9:48)

395. Do not be overcome by evil, but overcome evil with
good. (Rom. 12:21)

396. It does bother me. But if you ponder on it, you'd go
loony. You can't plan ahead, so you just live day-to-
day . . . It's not just the money. Work gives you
something to do. I'm just wasting away.

397. Society judges people many times by the work they do. So when we take people's jobs away we may be taking their status away as well.

398. 'Unemployment' is neither an unpredictable natural calamity nor yet an inevitable part of organised industry; it is simply the symptom of our collective inertia in the face of immediate challenge.

399. We believe that if men have the talent to invent new machines that put men out of work, they have the talent to put those men back to work.

400. When I was at school, I used to have loads of friends. Now a lot of them . . . have got jobs and you tend to lose contact. I've become lonely . . . I do get terribly depressed. At times I think I'll end it all, but I haven't got the nerve.

(f) Hymns and songs

401. *Responsorial Psalm – Psalm 145:*

Response: Come Lord, and save us.

It is he who keeps faith for ever
who is just to those who are oppressed.
It is he who gives bread to the hungry.
The Lord, who sets prisoners free.

The Lord who gives sight to the blind,
who raises up those who are bowed down,
the Lord, who protects the stranger
and upholds the widow and orphan.

It is the Lord who loves the just
but thwarts the path of the wicked.

The Lord will reign for ever,
Zion's God, from age to age.

402.   There in the bustees the drains are all choked;
The refuse is strewn on the street.
The children are playing in darkness and smoke
With nothing but mud on their feet.
They are so sure that nobody cares:
Don't give them doles in their hand!
They need their pride and their manhood rebuilt:
O, I do try to understand.

Chorus: You've got to do more than that (2)
Understanding is all very well,
But you've got to do more than that!

I hear the shouts and the din of the mob:
They've called out the policeman again.
Some want to save the life of the cow;
And some want to feed hungry men.
Some want a steel-plant: some want a State.
They're students, and folk of all kind:
I'm scared where it's leading: but what can I do?
So I'll leave it to those inclined!

Chorus: You've got to do more than that (2)
Leaving it to others is all very well,
But you've got to do more than that!

There once lived a man who was better than us:
With nowhere to lay down his head.
He went about lifting men from the mire:
Giving new life where manhood was dead.
They said he was dangerous: said he was mad.
With men who were sinners he sat;
Yet he gave himself for the life of the world:
And you can't do more than that.

CROSS-REFERENCE

(a) Service plans
(b) Daily manual of prayers and readings

CROSS-REFERENCE

(a) Service plans

The purpose of these service plans is not to provide a series of all-purpose services but rather to show how the various sections of the anthology may be brought together in a variety of ways.

(i) Theme: Creation and thanksgiving

Hymn: 347 ('The harvest of the city')

A. Creation

Sentence: 1 Cor. 3:9
Symbol presented (e.g. a picture of the earth taken from space)
Prayer: 30
Reading: John 1:1–14
Hymn: 335 ('God of fire and wind and water')

B. Confession

Sentence: Mark 8:26
Symbol broken (e.g. a picture of the earth ripped in half)
Prayer: 81
Hymn: 256 ('Creator of the earth and skies')

C. Repentance

Sentence: Rom. 12:2
Symbol restored (e.g. a picture of the earth stuck together)
Reading: 169 ('Encountering Light')
Hymn: 265 ('For the healing of the nations')

D. Thanksgiving

Sentence: Matt. 5:14,16
Symbol offered (e.g. a picture of the earth laid on the altar)
Prayer: 68

Concluding Prayer: 46
Hymn: 337 ('Great God of Town and City')
(The symbol used should be the focal point of the service and
the significance of the action in relation to the theme should
be explained at each stage.)

(ii) Theme: The responsibility of power

Hymn: 268 ('God is love, his the care')
Introductory prayer: 29

A. Confession: The misuse of power

Sentence: Mark 10:44
Prayer: 80
Reading: 188 ('The sharing of power')
Hymn: 258 ('Dear Lord and Father of mankind')

B. Dedication: The proper use of power

Prayer: 65
Reading: 164 ('Christian management')
Hymn: 239 ('All my hope on God is founded')

C. Service: The commitment to this proper use

Talk 1: (Christians in business talk of their experience of relating their faith to decision making)
Reading: John 13:3–17
Talk 2
Hymn: 342 ('Our song is of the city')
Talk 3
Concluding prayer: 59
Hymn: 266 ('Forth in thy name, O Lord, I go')

(iii) Theme: The right priorities

Sentence: Mic. 6:8
Hymn: 332 ('What does the Lord require')
Introductory prayer: 45
Confession: 77
Reading: 165 ('Christianity and human relations in industry')
Talk 1: Work is often a means to an end; for a Christian how work is organised is important too.
Hymn: 286 ('Lord Jesus Christ')
Reading: Eph. 4:17–32
Talk 2: For a Christian work should be based on the principle of love for all men, and business practice should be fair and just.
Hymn: 268 ('God is love, his the care')
Thanksgiving prayer: 96
Prayer: 9
Hymn: 334 ('Glory be to Thee, O God, Hallelujah')

(iv) Theme: Unemployment and commitment

Hymn: 301 ('O Jesus, I have promised')

A. Confession: The misuse of people

Sentence: 217
Prayer: 367
Reading: 383 ('Not wanted')
Talk on the theme of Confession
Hymn: 258 ('Dear Lord and Father of mankind')

B. Absolution: The value of people

Sentence: 203
Prayer: 363
Reading: 390 ('Unemployment is unacceptable')
Talk on the theme of Absolution
Hymn: 259 ('Father, hear the prayer we offer')

C. Commitment: The service of Christians

Sentence: Mark 10:44
Prayer: 59
Reading: Luke 10:25–37
Talk on the theme of Commitment
Hymn: 402 ('There in the bustees the drains are all choked')

(v) Theme: Unemployment, God suffers, God cares

Sentence: 396
Reading: 382 ('My last day')
Song: 341 ('O Lord, we can't see you')
Prayer: 361
Talk 1: The 'facts' of unemployment, e.g. 'signing on', 'limited amount of money'.
Reading: 385 ('Social and psychological well-being')
Prayer: 364

Talk 2: The 'facts' of unemployment, e.g. 'loss of friends', 'loss of meaning'.

Prayer: 369

Contemporary music: e.g. 'Gethsemane' from *Jesus Christ Superstar*

Reading: Mark 14:22–31, 34–39

Talk 3: Christ suffered, God suffered. God suffers, God cares.

Concluding prayer: 348

(Service plans *vi*, *vii* and *viii* are based around the Anglican ASB Rite A structure, but they may be easily adapted to the modern liturgies of the other major denominations.)

(vi) Theme: Creative work

Hymn: 338 ('In quest for knowledge, truth and skill')

Sentence: 234

Introductory prayers

Gloria

Collect: 2

Reading: 167 ('Creative work')

Hymn: 316 ('Servant of all, to toil for man')

Gospel: John 1:1–14

Talk: focused on four objects – a wood carving, a balance sheet, a pocket calculator and a picture of a power station – each to show that, in traditional crafts, commerce, new technology and heavy industry, workers create with God.

Creed

Litany: 86

Prayer of confession: 51

Peace

Offertory hymn: 288 ('Lord, look upon our working days')

Eucharistic prayer

Distribution

Concluding prayer

Blessing and dismissal
Hymn: 253 ('Come to us creative spirit')

(vii) Theme: Stewardship of God's Creation

Hymn: 263 ('For the beauty of the earth')
Sentence: Gen. 1:26
Introductory prayers
Gloria
Collect: 32
Reading: 176 ('Meditation on a sliced loaf')
Psalm 90
Gospel: Matt. 20:1–16
Talk: Slide series contrasting wealth and beauty with
poverty and squalor. All is God's creation but man
has spoilt and misused it.
Litany: 76
Peace
Offertory hymn: 264 ('For the fruits of His creation')
Eucharistic prayer
Distribution
Hymn: 345 ('The earth, the sky, the oceans')
Concluding prayers
Blessing and dismissal

(viii) Theme: The worker

Hymn: 254 ('Come, workers for the Lord')
Sentence: 235
Introductory prayers
Confession
Gloria
Collect: 70
Reading: 189 ('The worth of the worker')
Reading: Rom. 12:1–13
Hymn: 241 ('All who love and serve your city')
Gospel: Matt. 25:31–45

Sermon
Creed
Litany: 92
Peace
Offertory hymn: 339 ('Lord for the years your love')
Eucharistic prayer
Distribution
Sentence: 232
Hymn: 284 ('Lord as we rise to leave this shell of worship')
Concluding prayer: 71
Blessing and dismissal

(Service plans *ix* and *x* are intended to provide some examples of informal worship.)

(ix) Theme: God is active in the world

Hymn: 334 ('Glory be to Thee, O God')
Reading: 182 ('The Christian in industrial society')
Focus worship on an item, e.g. a newspaper, poster etc.
(Silence)
Each person says briefly how the item shows God working in the world.
Prayers: The leader draws together all these statements into prayers of intercession for the group.
Concluding prayer: 45

(x) Theme: Fellow creators with God

Service in the workplace

Take some item which goes through a number of processes – the ingredients for glass, paper, sheet metal – and follow it through the workplace. The Service begins and ends with a hymn and a prayer. At each stage a prayer and a reading are said.

Example: In a commercial office the Service could begin at a desk where the original business transaction is made.

Stage 1: The paper with the details may then be taken to the typist.

Stage 2: The typed letter is taken to the office manager.

Stage 3: It is carried to the post room.

Stage 4: It is taken by messenger out of the workplace.

The appropriateness of such a service and how it would be arranged in detail would depend entirely on those taking part, the particular work and the particular place. This is the attractiveness of this type of worship for, in being so closely tied, it has a particular relevance to a particular group of people.

(b) Daily manual of prayers and readings

This manual can be used by those who already use the lectionary by simply supplementing the prayer and reading. However, it can be used as a tool for daily prayer in itself by using the following structure:

Sentence
Reading
Lord's Prayer
Prayer
Period of silence for personal prayers
Concluding prayer 2

NOTE: The material on certain days concentrates on unemployment. These days are indicated by (UE) against each of the days concerned.

Week 1	Readings	Prayers
M	Neh. 4	1
T (UE)	Isa. 58:7–10	361
W	Matt. 5:14,16	76
T	Luke 12:13–34	3
F	167	51

Week 2	Readings	Prayers
M	Rev. 21:1–6	4
T	2 Chr. 5:1,13,14	5
W (UE)	397	173
T	Luke 10:25–28	6
F	340	56

Week 3		
M	1 John 4:7–21	7
T (UE)	381	362
W	Gen. 1:26	84
T	1 Chr. 29:1–13	8
F	168	66

Week 4		
M	Luke 4:14–21	9
T	1 Peter 2:4–12	10
W	129	96
T	Exodus 35:30–36:1	11
F	348	48

Week 5		
M	Matt. 25:31–45	12
T (UE)	Mark 14:22–31, 34–39	363
W	Rom. 15:1	85
T	James 4:13–5:12	13
F	176	52

Week 6		
M	Exod. 31:1–11	14
T	1 Thess. 5:12–33	77
W	Amos 5:14	15
T	Matt. 25:14–29	16
F	334	57

Week 7		
M	Exod. 18:13–23	17
T (UE)	382	364
W	218	86

Week 7 cont.	Readings	Prayers
T	Col. 3:1–17	18
F	182	67
Week 8		
M	Matt. 20:1–16	19
T	Exod. 1:8–14; 3:1–9	97
W	Job 38:4–7	20
T	Col. 1:11–20	21
F	Ps. 8	58
Week 9		
M	Matt. 18:21–35	22
T (UE)	Jer. 31:31–34	367
W	219	87
T	Deut. 26:1–11	23
F	178	68
Week 10		
M	Phil. 2:1–11	24
T	Matt. 7:1–12	25
W (UE)	396	369
T	Deut. 8:7–20	26
F	335	53
Week 11		
M	Eph. 6:5–12	27
T (UE)	383	361
W	1 Cor. 3:9	88
T	Matt. 6:24–34	28
F	181	59
Week 12		
M	Gen. 4:3–9	29
T	Eph. 4:17–32	30
W	220	78
T	Gen. 1:26–31a	31
F	Ps. 15	69

Week 13	Readings	Prayers
M	2 Cor. 8:1–14	32
T (UE)	Luke 10:25–37	362
W	Mic. 6:8	89
T	Gen. 1:1–end	33
F	183	60

Week 14		
M	Matt. 6:19–34	34
T	1 Cor. 15:49–58	35
W	221	98
T	Job 28:3–6, 9–15, 20, 23–28	36
F	336	70

Week 15		
M	Matt. 6:1–6	37
T (UE)	401	363
W	Ps. 85:12	90
T	1 Cor. 12:4–11	38
F	185	54

Week 16		
M	Prov. 3:1–6	39
T	John 1:1–14	40
W (UE)	398	368
T	Isa. 44:6–23	41
F	Ps. 9	61

Week 17		
M	1 Cor. 3:3–9	42
T (UE)	Lam. 3:19–33	364
W	222	91
T	Isa. 45:1–13	43
F	186	71

Week 18		
M	John 6:25–35	44
T	Isa. 58:7–10	45
W	1 Cor. 15:58	79

Week 18 cont.	*Readings*	*Prayers*
T	Rom. 13:1–10	46
F	337	62

Week 19		
M	Jer. 29:4–7	47
T (UE)	384	367
W	223	92
T	John 13:3–17	49
F	172	72

Week 20		
M	Ezek. 37:1–14	50
T	Rom. 12:1–13	1
W	Mark 8:36	99
T	Amos 5:6–15	3
F	Ps. 46	56

Week 21		
M	John 14:15–27	4
T (UE)	Luke 15:3–10	361
W	224	93
T	Amos 5:14–24	5
F	189	63

Week 22		
M	Rom. 8:14–17, 38–39	6
T	Mic. 4:1–7	7
W	Ps. 90:17	80
T	John 21:1–14	8
F	338	73

Week 23		
M	Acts 20:32–35	9
T (UE)	402	362
W	225	94
T	Mic. 6:6–8	10
F	191	64

Week 24	Readings	Prayers
M	Acts 1:15–26	11
T	Hab. 2:1–4, 9–14	12
W	2 Cor. 8:1–14	100
T	2 Thess. 3:16–18	13
F	Ps. 65	74

Week 25		
M	Phil. 4:4–7	14
T (UE)	Hosea 14:1, 2, 4–7	363
W	226	95
T	Luke 11:5–13	15
F	339	65

Week 26		
M	1 Kgs. 8:35–40	16
T	1 John 5:12–15	17
W	Mark 10:44	81
T	1 Tim. 6:6–10	18
F	164	75

Week 27		
M	Neh. 4	19
T (UE)	385	364
W	227	76
T	Rev. 21:1–6	20
F	Ps. 67	51

Week 28		
M	2 Chr. 5:1, 13, 14	21
T	Luke 10:25–28	22
W (UE)	399	370
T	1 John 4:7–21	23
F	169	56

Week 29		
M	1 Chr. 29:1–13	24
T	Luke 4:14–21	25
W	228	84

Week 29 cont.	*Readings*	*Prayers*
T	1 Peter 2:4–12	26
F	341	66
Week 30		
M	Exod. 35:30–36:1	27
T (UE)	Acts 2:42–47	367
W	Ps. 104:13, 15	96
T	Matt. 25:31–45	28
F	187	48
Week 31		
M	James 4:13–5:12	29
T	Exod. 31:1–11	30
W	229	85
T	1 Thess. 5:12–33	31
F	Ps. 90	52
Week 32		
M	Matt. 25:14–29	32
T (UE)	386	361
W	2 Cor. 9:6	77
T	Exod. 18:13–23	33
F	184	57
Week 33		
M	Col. 3:1–17	34
T	Mark 11:22–24	35
W	230	86
T	Deut. 28:1–14	36
F	342	67
Week 34		
M	Col. 1:11–20	37
T (UE)	Amos 5:4, 5, 10–13	362
W	Luke 6:37	97
T	Phil. 2:1–11	38
F	179	58

Week 35	Readings	Prayers
M	Matt. 7:1–12	39
T	Deut. 8:7–20	40
W	231	87
T	Eph. 6:5–12	41
F	Ps. 95	68

Week 36		
M	Matt. 6:24–34	42
T (UE)	388	363
W	Prov. 3:30–32	78
T	Eph. 4:17–32	43
F	165	53

Week 37		
M	Gen. 1:26–31a	44
T	2 Cor. 8:1–14	45
W (UE)	400	369
T	Job 28:3–6, 9–15, 20, 23–28	46
F	343	59

Week 38		
M	Matt. 6:19–34	47
T (UE)	Rom. 12:14–21	364
W	Gal. 6:7	88
T	Gen. 1:1–end	49
F	173	69

Week 39		
M	1 Cor. 15:49–58	50
T	Matt. 6:1–6	1
W	232	98
T	Prov. 3:1–6	3
F	Ps. 96	60

Week 40		
M	1 Cor. 12:4–11	4
T (UE)	Luke 12:13–34	367
W	Luke 14:11	89

Week 40 cont.	Readings	Prayers
T	Isa. 44:6–23	5
F	175	70

Week 41		
M	John 1:1–14	6
T	1 Cor. 3:3–9	7
W (UE)	Rom. 12:21	368
T	Isa. 45:1–13	8
F	344	54

Week 42		
M	John 6:25–35	9
T (UE)	Matt. 20:1–16	361
W	Eph. 4:31–32	90
T	Isa. 58:7–10	10
F	174	61

Week 43		
M	Rom. 13:1–10	11
T	Jer. 29:4–7	12
W	John 6:27	79
T	Ezek. 37:1–14	13
F	Ps. 100	71

Week 44		
M	John 13:3–17	14
T (UE)	390	362
W	233	91
T	Rom. 12:1–13	15
F	188	62

Week 45		
M	Amos 5:6–15	16
T	John 14:15–27	17
W	Phil. 4:4	99
T	Rom. 8:14–17, 38–39	18
F	345	72

Week 46	Readings	Prayers
M	Amos 5:14–24	19
T (UE)	Gen. 4:3–9	363
W	234	92
T	Mic. 4:1–7	20
F	190	55

Week 47		
M	John 21:1–14	21
T	Acts 20:32–35	22
W	Rom. 12:2	80
T	Mic. 6:6–8	23
F	Ps. 104:1–25	63

Week 48		
M	Acts 1:15–26	24
T (UE)	Exod. 1:8–14; 3:1–9	364
W	235	93
T	Hab. 2:1–4, 9–14	25
F	177	73

Week 49		
M	2 Cor. 8:14	26
T	2 Thess. 3:6–13	27
W	Col. 3:15	100
T	Phil. 4:4–7	28
F	346	64

Week 50		
M	Mark 11:22–24	29
T	Deut. 28:1–14	30
W	236	94
T	Luke 11:5–13	31
F	180	74

Week 51		
M	1 Kgs. 8:35–40	32
T (UE)	389	367
W	Luke 12:34	81

Week 51 cont.	*Readings*	*Prayers*
T	1 John 5:12–15	33
F	Ps. 107:23–32	65
Week 52		
M	1 Tim. 6:6–10	34
T	Matt. 18:21–35	35
W	Lam. 3:22–23	95
T	Deut. 26:1–11	36
F	347	75

FURTHER RESOURCES

(a) Anthology material
(b) Bibliography
(c) Cathedral services
(d) Denominations
(e) Organisations
(f) Worship aids

FURTHER RESOURCES

(a) Anthology material

The worship material included in this anthology represents about one third of the total material available to the compiler. The entire collection of services and suggestions for worship is fully indexed and kept in the library of Sion College in London. The material is available for anyone to consult, in arrangement with the Librarian. The following short bibliography is deliberately restricted to the more unusual sources in order to highlight them.

(b) Bibliography

(i) For preparing services

Appleton, G., *In his name*, Lutterworth.
Knight, Rev. A. G., *Joyful journey*, Toc H.
Ogden, B., and Watt, E., *Christian family festivals*, C.I.O.
Quoist, M., *Prayers of life*, Gill and Macmillan.
Smith, R., and Forster, J., *Industrial festivals! . . . What, at my church?* Methodist Church in Industry Committee, Home Mission Division.
Williams, E., ed., *Prayers for Today's Church*, C.P.A.S.

(ii) For understanding the link between work and worship

Kane, M., *Theology in an industrial society*, S.C.M., 1975.
Pope John Paul II, Encyclical *Laborem Exercens*, 1981.
Taylor, M., *Variations on a Theme*, Galliard, 1977.
Wilkie, G., *Christian thinking about industrial life*, St. Andrews Press, Edinburgh.

(c) Cathedral services

In recent years some Anglican cathedrals have been holding Industrial Sunday services. The following are the most helpful to approach about this:

The Provost,
The Provost's House,
8 Davenport Road,
Coventry,
West Midlands,
CVS 6PU

The Dean of Guildford,
The Deanery,
1 Cathedral Close,
Guildford,
Surrey.

The Dean of Rochester,
The Deanery,
Kings Orchard,
Rochester,
Kent,
ME1 1TG

The Provost of Sheffield,
Provost's Lodge,
22 Hallam Gate Road,
Sheffield,
South Yorkshire,
SI0 5BS

The Dean of St Paul's,
The Deanery,
9 Amen Court,
London,
EC4M 7BU

(d) Denominations

The various major denominations of the Church have central committees which may be able to provide some information and which can supply the names and addresses of local people and organisations.

(i) Church of England

The Board for Social Responsibility,
Church House,
Dean's Yard,
London,
SW1P 3NZ

Most dioceses also have their own local boards and industrial mission teams, whose names and addresses are always available from the Church of England's Yearbook, published annually by C.I.O.

(ii) Church of Scotland

The Church of Scotland Home Board,
121 George Street,
Edinburgh,
EH2 4YN

The Board has produced two helpful leaflets entitled *Prayers suitable for a Festival of Daily Work* and *Suggestions for a 'Festival of Daily Work'.*

(iii) Methodist Church

Home Mission Department,
Methodist Church,
1 Central Buildings,
Westminster,
London,
SW1 1NU

The Department has produced an excellent leaflet, previously mentioned, *Industrial festivals! . . . What, at my Church?*

(iv) Roman Catholic Church

The Secretary,
The World of Work Committee,
38/40 Eccleston Square,
London,
SW1V 1PD

'Action in Work Service' and 'Young Christian Workers' are
two Roman Catholic organisations and their addresses are
given on pages 191 and 193 respectively.

(v) Society of Friends

The Secretary,
Industry and Work Committee,
Friends House,
Euston Road,
London,
NW1 2BJ

(vi) The Baptist Union

Department of Ministry,
Baptist Union of Great Britain and Ireland,
Baptist Church House,
4 Southampton Row,
London,
WC1B 4AB

(vii) United Reformed Church

Church and Society Department,
The United Reformed Church,
86 Tavistock Place,
London,
WC1H 9RT

(e) Organisations

(i) Action in Work Service, F.S.A.

120b, West Heath Road,
London, NW3

F.S.A. produces a variety of pamphlets and booklets,
including *Our Parish and Unemployment.*

(ii) European Christian Industrial Movement

37 Westmoreland Terrace,
London, SW1

(iii) Evangelical Coalition for Urban Mission

Scripture Union House,
130 City Road,
London,
EC1V 2NJ

(iv) Industrial Christian Fellowship

St Katherine Cree Church,
86 Leadenhall Street,
London, EC3

The I.C.F. publishes a quarterly magazine which provides a great deal of interesting and helpful information.

(v)   Industrial Mission Association

This has local branches throughout the country. It produces a monthly newsletter which contains many original pieces and is available from:

> The Editor,
> Industrial Mission Association Newsletter,
> 55 Greylands Avenue,
> Norton,
> Stockton-on-Tees,
> Cleveland,
> TS20 2PA

(vi)   Luton Industrial College

> Chapel Street,
> Luton,
> LU1 2SE

The College has published a useful leaflet, *Suggestions for Industrial Festivals*, and runs many excellent courses throughout the year on various aspects of Christianity in the secular world.

(vii)   The Industrial Society

> Common Purpose Campaign,
> Peter Runge House,
> 3 Carlton House Terrace,
> London,
> SW1Y 5DG

The Society annually publishes sermon notes, for Industrial Sunday, which may be useful not only for preachers but also to guide discussions in groups.

(viii)   William Temple Association

> Liddon House,
> 24 South Audley Street,
> London W1

(ix)   William Temple Foundation

> Manchester Business School,
> Manchester,
> MI5 6PB

(x)   Workers Christian Fellowship

> 40 Balmoral Road,
> Watford,
> Herts.
> WD2 4EP

(xi)   Urban Theology Unit

> 210 Abbeyfield,
> Sheffield,
> S4 7AZ

> The Unit publishes many helpful booklets which are reasonably priced.

(xii)   Young Christian Workers

> 2 Garden Close,
> London, SW9

(f) Worship aids

(i) The U.S.P.G. has produced an excellent series of thought-provoking posters and filmstrips. These are available at a variety of prices from:

15 Tufton Street,
Westminster,
London,
SW1P 3QQ

(ii) Newspaper cuttings, radio and television programmes – thoughtfully selected and used – can provide a stimulating alternative to a sermon. Many firms produce lavish publicity material which can also be used.

INDEXES

(a) Theme index
(b) Index of non-biblical sources

INDEXES

(a) Theme index

The abbreviations used in this Index represent the sections of the anthology, for example: RB – *b* = 'Readings: Biblical', part *b*.

The abbreviations used are as follows:
P = Prayers   L = Litanies
RB = Readings: biblical   RNB = Readings: non-biblical
S = Sentences   HS = Hymns and songs

Co-creators with God

Community

Confession

P   – 51–55
L   – 76–81
RB   – *b* (iii)
RNB – 168, 176, 180, 186
S   – *a* Job 38:4–7; Prov. 3:30–32; 2 Cor. 9:6
     – *b* 218
HS   – *c* Ps. 90
     – *d* (i)

Creation

P   – 30, 37, 69
L   – 85, 96
RB   – *b* (ii); *b* (ix)
RNB – 167, 171, 172, 187, 191
S   – *a* Gen. 1:26; Job 38:4–7; Ps. 85:12; 1 Cor. 3:9
     – *b* 217, 226
HS   – *b* 335, 336, 347
     – *c* Pss. 19, 95; 104:1–25
     – *d* (iii)

Daily work

P   – 2, 7, 9, 12, 26, 42, 48, 72
L   – 89, 95, 96
RB   – *b* (i); *b* (iv); *b* (v)
RNB – 169, 174, 177, 182
S   – *a* Ps. 90:17; Mark 8:36; John 6:27; Eph. 4:31–32
     – *b* 217, 219, 223, 232, 234, 235
HS   – *b* 337, 340
     – *c* Ps. 15

Dangerous and unpleasant work

P   – 20, 25, 40, 47
L   – 90, 91, 92, 93

Justice

```
P     – 7, 18, 24, 28, 44, 45
L     – 81, 88
RB    – b (i), (iv), (x)
RNB – 168
S     – a  Mic. 6:8; Rom. 12:2; 2 Cor. 9:6; Gal. 6:7
      – b  218, 227, 228
HS    – b  342, 343, 346
      – d  (ix)
```

Service

```
P     – 1, 3, 8, 11, 13, 14, 17, 27, 36, 41, 43, 50, 56–65, 75
L     – 77, 78, 87, 90
RB    – b (x)
RNB – 166, 169, 170, 172, 175, 177, 179, 180, 181, 187, 190
S     – a  Gen. 1:26; Matt. 5:14,16; Mark 10:44; Luke 6:37;
             Rom. 12:2, 15:1
      – b  222, 225, 227, 233
HS    – b  344, 345
      – d  (ii), (v), (vii)
```

Stewardship

```
P     – 31, 32, 33, 34, 35, 37, 49, 51, 68, 73
L     – 76, 79, 85, 87, 88, 91, 95, 96
RB    – b (ii), (iii)
RNB – 176, 186, 190
S     – a  Gen. 1:26; Pss. 85:12; 104:13, 15; 2 Cor. 8:14
HS    – b  345
      – c  Pss. 8, 90
```

Suffering

```
P     – 14, 16, 19, 51
L     – 76
RB    – b (viii)
```

Thanksgiving

Those who lead

Unemployment

See last section of the anthology, pages 143–164.

(b) Index of non-biblical sources

I wish to thank all who have granted permission for the use of various non-biblical items in this anthology. Every effort has been made to correctly identify all the items. If these acknowledgements err in any way or unwittingly infringe copyright, I apologise sincerely and will make corrections in any further editions.

The references to biblical quotations (all from the Revised Standard Version, copyright 1946, 1952, 1971 and 1973 by Division of Christian Education of the National Council of the Churches of Christ in the United States of America) are given in the anthology as they occur – unlike the non-biblical quotations, whose sources are given only in this Index. The numbers here correspond to the non-biblical quotations as they appear in the anthology.

1. Canon Alan Christmas.
2. I.C.F.
3. From 'A Service at which the Marlow Declaration will be offered in Westminster Abbey', May 19th, 1963.
4. I.C.F.
5. Adapted from a prayer taken from *Prayers for the City of God*, author and publisher unknown.
6. As 5.
7. From 'People Matter', Rochester Cathedral, May 15th, 1983.
8. From 'A Service of Dedication on the occasion of the amalgamation of the Royal Institution of Chartered Surveyors with the Chartered Land Agents' Society and the Chartered Auctioneers' and Estate Agents' Institute', Coventry Cathedral, July 1st, 1970.
9. From 'A Service in Praise of Craftsmen', Coventry Cathedral, November 20th, 1965.
10. From *Prayers suitable for a Festival of Daily Work*, Church of Scotland Home Mission Board.
11. C.J.B.
12. Rev. A. G. Knight, from *Joyful Journey: Patterns of Prayer in Toc H*.
13. From *You have a minute, Lord?* by David Kossoff, published by Robson Books Ltd.
14. C.J.B.
15. From Christian Education Movement Conference, 'Why can't you see conflict my way?' November 6th, 1982.
16. 'Found on a scrap of wrapping paper beside the body of a dead child in Ravensbruck concentration camp', taken from *Joyful Journey* (see 12, above).
17. C.J.B.
18. Adapted from I.C.F. Prayer Card.
19. As 18.
20. As 3.
21. 'A Service for the Royal Institute of British Architects', Coventry Cathedral, July 12th, 1962.

22. Reinhold Niebuhr.
23. I.C.F.
24. As 12.
25. C.J.B.
26. C.J.B.
27. C.J.B.
28. Rev. R. M. Benson.
29. C.J.B.
30. I.C.F.
31. I.C.F.
32. Adapted, I.C.F.
33. As 5.
34. I.C.F.
35. Rev. C. R. Smith, from *Opening Prayers at the Conference on the Impact of New Technology*.
36. As 35.
37. From 'Service of Commissioning and Welcoming of Deaconess June Winfield', London Industrial Chaplaincy, April 19th, 1983.
38. From *Suggestions for an Order of Service for Industrial Festivals*, Luton Industrial College.
39. Sir Edward Maufe.
40. I.C.F.
41. From 'Service for the Guild of Cordwainers', Coventry Cathedral, October 14th, 1976.
42. Bishop Westcott.
43. I.C.F.
44. Rev. C. R. Smith, from *Methodist Conference Prayers*, June 23rd, 1979.
45. Rev. Paul Brett.
46. From *Suggestions for a Service on the Theme of 'Work'*, Coventry Industrial Mission.
47. Canon P. Dearmer.
48. From 'Service of Dedication', Leeds Industrial Mission, January 27th, 1981.
49. I.C.F.
50. Adapted from prayer by Canon Alan Christmas.
51. From 'Service of Dedication', Leeds Industrial Mission, March 9th, 1982.
52. As 44.
53. Rev. John Foster, from 'Industrial Festival Evening Service', All Saints', Darlaston.
54. As 38.

55. Rev. John Forster, from 'Industrial Festival Service', George Street Methodist Church, Ettingshall, December 11th, 1977.
56. From 'Industrial Festival Service', Rochester Cathedral, March 12th, 1961.
57. I.C.F.
58. As 38.
59. From 'A Service of Thanksgiving and Intercession for British Industry and Commerce 1982', St Paul's Cathedral.
60. I.C.F.
61. I.C.F.
62. As 10.
63. As 38.
64. From 'Annual Service of Thanksgiving and Rededication 1982', South London Industrial Mission (S.L.I.M.).
65. From 'Annual Service of Thanksgiving and Rededication 1980', S.L.I.M.
66. As 59.
67. I.C.F.
68. As 53.
69. As 38.
70. As 44.
71. As 51.
72. From *New Every Morning*, B.B.C. Publications, p.79.
73. Rev. Trevor Parkin, from *Earning our Daily Bread*, Middleton Hall, Milton Keynes, September 30th, 1979.
74. As 73.
75. Prayers adapted from 73.
76. I.C.F.
77. From 'Lloyds Bank Ltd. Annual Service', May 13th, 1980.
78. From *Eucharist of the Radical Christ*, Urban Theology Unit.
79. As 41.
80. As 56.
81. From 'Annual Service of the London Industrial Chaplaincy', May 18th, 1982.
82. I.C.F.
83. From *Worship Material for Rogation/Industrial Sunday 1977*, Industry, Trade and Employment Mission (I.T.E.M.), Reading.
84. 'Festival Service for Commerce and Industry, 1972', Coventry Cathedral, November 12th, 1972.
85. Rev. Philip Lee-Bapty, *Litany for Industry and Commerce*, Coventry Industrial Mission.

86. From 'The Licensing of the Reverend Barry Etherington', September 10th, 1978, Herefordshire and Bedfordshire Industrial Council.

87. As 77.

88. From *Work and Worship*, St. Mary's Parish Church, St. Neots, April 20th, 1980.

89. I.C.F.

90. From the 'Annual Thanksgiving Service', S.L.I.M., October 23rd, 1963.

91. As 10.

92. From 'The Commissioning of Kenneth Cox', Liverpool Industrial Mission, April 10th, 1981.

93. *Intercessions for Industrial Life*, by Rev. C. R. Smith.

94. As 44.

95. *Prayer with Responses*, by Canon Alan Christmas.

96. I.C.F.

97. As 84.

98. I.C.F.

99. As 86.

100. From an 'Industrial Service', West Slough Parish, 1979.

164. Extract from 'Christians in Management', a lecture given by Mr George Goyder, Chairman, British International Paper Ltd., in the Guild Church of St Katherine Cree, Leadenhall Street, London EC3, on November 29th, 1967.

165. Extract from *Christianity and Human Relations in Industry*, by Sir George Schuster, Epworth Press, London, 1951, pp.19, 20.

166. Extract from *Industrial Sunday Sermon Notes, 1978*, The Industrial Society.

167. From 44.

168. Extract from *Christianity and Social Order*, by William Temple, Shepherd-Walwyn (Publishers) Ltd.; first published 1942.

169. Extract from *Encountering Light*, by Gonville ffrench-Beytagh, Collins, 1975.

170. Author unknown.

171. 'Reflections on Things', by John Davis, *I.C.F. Quarterly*, Spring 1984.

172. 'He took bread', by Kenneth Adams, *I.C.F. Quarterly*, Spring 1984.

173. Extract from *Small is Beautiful*, by E. F. Schumacher, Abacus, 1972.

174. Extract from *Laborem Exercens*, Catholic Truth Society, S 355.

175. Extract from *Industrial Sunday Sermon Notes, May 1982*, by Rev. Malcolm Grundy, The Industrial Society.

176. 'Meditations on a Sliced Loaf', by Piers Nash Williams, *Oxford Diocesan Magazine*.

177. 'Are Computers Taking Over?', by John Wren-Lewis, I.C.F. lecture, November 22nd, 1967.

178. 'Through Faith to Freedom', by Dyfan Thomas, *Broadsheet*, I.C.F.

179. From 86.

180. *A Christian Front in Industry*, author unknown.

181. *Training for Non-Professionalised, Non-Stipendiary, Lay Ministry*, by Miss Ruth Etchells.

182. 'The Christian in Industrial Society', by E. F. Schumacher, *I.C.F. Quarterly*, April 1963.

183. Extract from 'The Christian View of the Right Relationship between Finance, Production and Consumption', by William Temple. Lecture given at the Central Hall, Westminster, February 4th, 1943.

184. Extract from 'The Church and the World Economic Crisis', by Sir Stafford Cripps, *Broadsheet*, I.C.F.

185. 'Presidential Address by the Bishop of Ripon', Ripon Diocesan Synod, June 1978.

186. Extract from 'The Meaning of Worship', by J. V. Wilson, *Broadsheet*, I.C.F.

187. As 171.

188. *A Christian Approach to Industrial Democracy*, by Clifford Cleal, Department of Mission of the Baptist Union.

189. As 166.

190. 'The Adventure of Life', by G. A. Studdert Kennedy, from *The Torch*, September 1926.

191. Author unknown.

217. M. Kane, *Theology in an Industrial Society*, S.C.M., 1975, p.3.

218. Father Thomas Cullinan, O.S.B.

219. As 173.

220. Mother Teresa of Calcutta.

221. St Thomas Aquinas.

222. Anon.

223. As 183.

224. A Bucks refuse collector.

225. Author unknown.
226. Booker T. Washington from the Atlanta Exposition, September 1895. Quotation from *International Thesaurus of Quotations*, J. B. Lippincott, George Allen and Unwin.
227. From *The Form of the Church*, by A. G. Hebert.
228. John F. Kennedy, May 1963; as 138.
229. As 174.
230. Author unknown.
231. From *Christianity and Industrial Problems*, the Report of the Archbishop's Fifth Committee of Inquiry, 1918.
232. As 231.
233. William Temple.
234. From *Science and Human Values*, by Jacob Bronowski. As 226.
235. As 182.
236. As 174.

334. ASIA – Tune: Easter Hymn.
335. Rev. J. Pearce-Higgins – Tune: Austria.
336. Fred Kahn © Stainer and Bell Ltd. – Tune: Darwall's 148th.
337. Derek Nuttal – Tune: Aurelia.
338. Alan Ogie © Stainer and Bell Ltd. – Tune: Martham.
339. Timothy Dudley-Smith – Tune: Welwyn.
340. Fred Pratt Green © Stainer and Bell Ltd. – Tune: Crofts 148th or Christchurch.
341. As 334.
342. As 334.
343. Fred Kahn © Stainer and Bell Ltd.
344. Fred Kahn © Stainer and Bell Ltd.
345. From 'Annual Service of the London Industrial Chaplaincy, May 1982' – Tune: Thornbury.
346. As 334.
347. Sydney Carter © Stainer and Bell Ltd. – Tune: Pflügen.
348. G. A. Studdert-Kennedy – Tune: Lombard Street.

361. From 'Unemployment Vigil', St. Philip's Cathedral, Birmingham.
362. As 361.
363. As 10.
364. C.J.B.
365. C.J.B.
366. C.J.B.

367.	From *Our Parish and Unemployment*, F.S.A. World of Work Service.
368.	As 367.
369.	C.J.B.
370.	C.J.B.

381.	Rev. Philip Lee-Bapty, from *Coventry Industrial Newsletter*, No. 16, February/March 1981.
382.	Godfrey Fletcher from *Industrial Mission Association Newsletter*.
383.	Extract from 'Not Wanted' by Stephan Hopkinson, *I.C.F. Quarterly*, April 1963.
384.	Rev. Martin Wright from *Coventry Industrial Mission Newsletter*, Christmas 1981.
385.	Extract from 'Long-Term Unemployment', *Youthaid Bulletin*, June 1980.
386.	As 381.
387.	Extract from *God, Man and Society*, by V. A. Demant, S.C.M., 1933.
388.	'The End of a Work-Based Society?' David Welbourn from *Mission in Industrial Society*, papers from the Industrial Mission Association in Britain for a conference at the Selly Oak Colleges, Birmingham, July 13–15th, 1978.
389.	Canon Alan Christmas.
390.	Author unknown.

396.	As 385.
397.	From *Unemployment*, by Fr. Peter Fitzgibbon, S.L.I.M., December 1980.
398.	As 383.
399.	John F. Kennedy. As 138.
400.	As 385.
401.	As 367.
402.	As 334.